Weaving It Together

Connecting Reading and Writing

Second Edition

Teaching Hints and Answer Key
Language Summary
Assessment Questions
Video Scripts

Milada Broukal • John Chapman • Patricia Brenner

THOMSON ™

HEINLE

Australia • Canada • Mexico • Singapore • United Kingdom • United States

**Weaving It Together: Connecting Reading and Writing
Instructor's Manual, Books 3 and 4/ Second Edition**
Milada Broukal, John Chapman, and Patricia Brenner

Publisher, Adult and Academic ESL: James W. Brown
Sr. Acquisitions Editor: Sherrise Roehr
Sr. Developmental Editor: Ingrid Wisniewska
Assistant Editor: Audra Longert
Sr. Production Editor: Maryellen Killeen
Sr. Marketing Manager: Charlotte Sturdy
Sr. Print Buyer: Mary Beth Hennebury
Project Manager: Lifland et al., Bookmakers
Compositor: Parkwood Composition
Cover Designer: Rotunda Design/Gina Petti
Interior Designer: Quica Ostrander/Lifland et al., Bookmakers
Printer: West Group

Printed in the United States of America
2 3 4 5 6 7 8 9 10   08 07 06 05 04

For more information contact Heinle, 25 Thomson Place, Boston, MA 02210 USA,
or you can visit our Internet site at http://www.heinle.com

For permission to use material from this text or product contact us:
Tel   1-800-730-2214
Fax   1-800-730-2215
Web www.thomsonrights.com

ISBN: 0-8384-4821-6

Cover photos: (top) Bonnie Kamin/Index Stock Imagery; (bottom) Carl Rosenstein/Index Stock Imagery

Contents

To the Teacher

Organization of the Student Book

Weaving It Together, Book 3, has eight units. Each unit is divided into two chapters related to the unit theme. *Weaving It Together, Book 4* has nine chapters. Each chapter has two readings related to a single chapter theme. The themes have been carefully selected to appeal to a wide range of interests and to promote discussion and comparison of different cultures. Unit and chapter opener pictures provide a visual stimulus to start off discussion. The readings provide input intended to generate a variety of responses, and students should be encouraged to ask further questions about the readings and to question their own and each other's opinions in an open and constructive way. These ideas are later expanded through vocabulary, comprehension, and discussion activities and lead to writing tasks that grow naturally out of the previous reading and discussion.

The sequence of activities in each chapter follows this pattern:

*   Predicting and pre-reading questions or activity
*   Reading
*   Vocabulary
*   Comprehension
*   Discussion
*   Writing skills
*   Writing practice

Each step in the sequence is important to the final goal of enabling students to produce excellent written English. All skills of reading, writing, generating ideas, and developing vocabulary are integrated throughout each chapter, with the aim of achieving this goal. See the sample lesson plans on pages 1–6 for suggestions on timing and how to use each stage of the lesson.

Grading of Written Work

The criteria you choose for grading your students' written work will vary according to the aims in your course description. In general, your students can be expected to hand in at least one preliminary draft of their work before handing in their final draft. The process of re-writing and editing written work is consistently emphasized in this series. The editing tips at the end of each section will help students become effective editors of their own and each other's work. It is also important to value original and thoughtful writing, as well as the amount of effort invested in the work.

Here are some suggestions for correcting students' written work:

*   Use written correction symbols so that students have to find their own mistakes (see page 8 for examples). You may want to provide students with a

list of these symbols so that they can refer to them when you hand back their work.

- Make clear your criteria for grading written work. You may want to use the same criteria each time, or you may prefer to focus on specific points. You might focus on paragraph formatting for the first assignment, for example, and then gradually add other criteria such as grammar, vocabulary, and content. See page 9 for possible writing rubrics, which may be adapted for your class.

- Have students work in pairs to check their essays before handing them in. Peer editing is a great way to help students learn to become more independent. Encourage students to use the editing checklist at the end of each chapter in the student book when correcting each other's work.

- Remember that a page covered in corrections is going to be very discouraging for your students. Try to limit the number of corrections you make by using correction symbols and by focusing only on errors that impede meaning or only on the grammar or organizational points taught in the chapter. If one mistake recurs frequently in an essay, correct it just once and ask the student to find other examples of the mistake by himself or herself.

- Remember to use a balance of both praise and criticism in your comments!

Journals

Journals provide an effective way of increasing the value of class time, as they encourage learning out of class. Students can experiment with new language they have recently learned or read, prepare their thoughts about a topic before discussing it in class, or respond in a personal way to the topics that are discussed in class. Journals are especially effective with shy or quiet students, who may not feel comfortable speaking out in class. They are also an excellent way for you to get direct feedback from students as to how well they have understood a lesson and what their feelings are about the topics under discussion. Journals allow teachers to communicate directly with individual students on a regular basis.

Not all students will find it easy to write a journal. Some may not be used to this type of writing; others may wish to have every word corrected by the teacher. It is important to explain your goals and the purpose of the journal in your course.

There is no doubt that the use of journals creates extra work for the teacher! Be realistic about how much time you can spend on reading and responding to your students' journal writing. However, the more enthusiastic you are about journals, the better your students will respond, and you may find yourself learning a great deal that will ultimately help you to understand your students better and aid you in your classroom teaching. Suggestions for journal writing tasks are given throughout this manual in the Teaching Hints section for each chapter. Additionally, you may ask students to write about what kind of class activities they enjoy most or find most useful or to write about how they feel their writing skills are progressing.

Following are some suggestions for using journals in your class:

- Use journals for free writing. Do not correct spelling, grammar, or other errors. The purpose of journals is to generate ideas that will be used later in more formal writing assignments.

- Respond with brief supportive comments that show you appreciate the writer's feelings as an individual, or engage in dialogue with the student by asking questions about what has been written.

- Provide a model journal entry to show students the length and the type of writing you expect to see.

- Bring in a notebook or notebook paper to demonstrate what format you would like the journal to be presented in.
- State your criteria for grading journals at the beginning of the semester. You may find it sufficient if students complete the required number of journal entries, or you may want to grade effort or relevance to course material. It is important that these criteria be clear to your students before they begin journal writing.
- Set a fixed number of journal entries and a fixed number of times for journals to be handed in over the semester. If journal writing is a requirement, students may leave it to the last minute and try to write all their journal entries in the last week of the semester!
- Establish that journal writing is personal and will not be shown to other students. Alternatively, you may ask students to choose a journal writing partner, with whom they can exchange journals. This allows more independence from the teacher, but is more difficult to monitor.

Video Activity

At the end of each section is a video activity related to the videotapes that accompany this series. Showing videos is a fun way to bring media into the classroom, to allow students to experience authentic spoken English in a variety of contexts, and to appeal to different learning styles. The video activity is optional and can be used to expand vocabulary or develop ideas. The final question in the video activity can be used independently of the video for discussion or as a springboard for further writing.

Internet Activity

Also at the end of each unit is an Internet activity, which gives students the opportunity to develop their Internet research skills. This activity can be done in a classroom setting with the guidance of the teacher or, if students have Internet access, as a homework task leading to a classroom presentation or discussion. At first, students may find searching the Internet very time-consuming. Encourage students to share tips and advice on how to search. The Internet activities are designed to help students develop a critical approach to information obtained on the Internet. We have not suggested any specific web sites, but the Teaching Hints provide suggested keywords to be used with a search engine, as well as additional activity ideas. Go to

www.heinle.wit

to find out more about how do an Internet search.

Note: Remember that not all web sites provide accurate information. Students should be advised to compare a few web sites to help verify data. Be careful to warn students of the dangers of giving up any personal information to web sites or downloading any files from unknown sources.

Each chapter in *Weaving It Together, Book 3*, follows a carefully designed sequence of activities, which guides students through the process of connecting reading to writing. Each chapter takes approximately 2 hours of class time.

Lesson 1 (60 minutes)

1. **Unit photo and warm-up (10 minutes).** The unit opens with one or more photos reflecting the theme of the unit. Use the photos to ask questions related to the general theme and to gather ideas to be used later in the two chapters. The Teaching Hints for each chapter give additional information related to the chapter theme and creative ways of introducing the theme, thereby activating the visual, audio, and kinesthetic learning styles of students.

2. **Chapter photo and pre-reading questions (5 minutes).** Use the chapter photo and pre-reading questions to introduce the specific theme of the chapter. Activating students' background knowledge of the topic will make the readings easier to understand.

3. **Predicting (5 minutes).** This activity helps students focus more closely on the material they will meet in the reading. The aim of the predicting activity is not to find the correct answers (though they may check the answers after doing the reading), but to develop the skill of anticipating what the text is going to be about by looking at a few key items. The predicting activity in Unit 2, for example, encourages students to guess which of the words are in the reading; the one in Unit 4 encourages students to guess what the story is about by looking at a few of the key words.

4. **Vocabulary and comprehension questions (25 minutes).** To encourage rapid and effective reading skills, you may wish to follow this pattern:
   a. Ask students two or three easy comprehension questions that guide them to the main points of the reading (see the Teaching Hints for suggested questions). Set a time limit of about 3 minutes for students to find the answers quickly.
   b. Have students read the Vocabulary Meaning questions, work in pairs to answer them, and then go back to the reading to check their answers. Have students work in pairs to answer the Vocabulary Word Building questions and then compare their answers as a group. Can they think of any additional word forms for each of the vocabulary items?
   c. Have students read the general comprehension questions (Looking for the Main Ideas), and set a time limit of 3 minutes for a second reading of the passage. Then give students 10 minutes to write the answers or discuss them in pairs. Have them check the answers by referring back to the passage.
   d. Give students a chance to search for and guess the meanings of any unknown words. Then ask students to answer the detailed comprehension questions (Looking for Details) and the questions about Making Inferences and Drawing Conclusions, referring back to the passage for the answers.

    e. Use the Teaching Hints for additional ideas on using the reading and extending the comprehension activity.

5. **Discussion (15 minutes).** The discussion questions give students a chance to respond to the readings on a personal level by relating the theme to their own concerns and giving their own opinions. The result is a deeper processing of the material, which will help students remember the vocabulary and the theme and develop ideas to use in their writing later. You may assign students to summarize ideas from the discussion for homework.

Lesson 2 (60 minutes)

1. **Review (5 minutes).** Review the vocabulary and themes from the first part of the chapter. Extend the vocabulary to include words and phrases related to students' own cultural context, if appropriate. Encourage students to keep a systematic record of new vocabulary in a notebook or on cards, adding definitions and example sentences to help them remember. Check answers to homework.

2. **Writing skills (15 minutes).** Present the new grammar or organizational writing point to be practiced in this lesson. Set a time limit for students to complete the guided writing exercises. Allow plenty of time so that all students are able to complete the task. Encourage students to read each other's work and offer comments. Call on students to write their sentences on the board, and invite constructive criticism from the rest of the class.

3. **Writing practice (20 minutes).** Get students started on their essay by having them choose a title and brainstorm ideas. Those who work fast can start writing; those who need more time to develop ideas may discuss in pairs or groups. (Note: Essays are assigned starting in Chapter 5 of Book 3.)

4. **Quiz, video activity, or Internet activity (20 minutes).** At the end of each unit, you will find a fun quiz, a video activity, and an Internet activity. These are all optional and may be used at different stages of the unit, as appropriate. Depending on the theme, you may want to show the video with the first chapter in a unit, for example, or you may want to assign the Internet task as homework and then use it to review the unit in your next lesson.

    a. The quiz can serve as a nice conclusion to a unit. You may want to organize it as a team competition or as pair work. You could also ask students to create similar quizzes based on the theme of the unit.

    b. When you show videos, we recommend that you encourage students to listen and watch for the general meaning only. Play the tapes as often as required for students to be able to complete the task. We do not recommend that you use the video for detailed listening comprehension. The scripts for the videos are provided at the end of this manual.

    c. One of the aims of Internet activities is to provide students with an opportunity to develop the skills needed for independent study. These tasks, therefore, are designed for students to complete on their own time, bringing the results of their research to class for discussion or using the information in their writing. Encourage students to share tips and advice on how to search and to be critical of the information they obtain. Advise students to use a search engine such as **www.google.com** or **www.yahoo.com**. Suggestions for alternative keywords are given in the Teaching Hints. *Note:* Be careful to warn students of the dangers of giving up any personal information to web sites or downloading any files from unknown sources.

5. **Journal (optional).** The journal can be used in a variety of ways—as a personal record the student uses for brainstorming ideas; as a dialogue between the teacher and the student; as a class journal, in which each member of the

class takes a turn writing his or her opinions and ideas. However you decide to use the journal, you will find many suggestions for journal writing topics in the Teaching Hints.

6. **Assessment (60 minutes).** You will find an assessment for each chapter at the end of this manual. The assessment consists of the following:

   a. Ten multiple-choice questions on vocabulary (30 points)

   b. Ten multiple-choice questions on the grammar, punctuation, or writing skills found in the chapter (30 points)

   c. An essay question (40 points)

Each chapter in *Weaving It Together, Book 4,* follows a carefully designed sequence of activities, which guides students through the process of connecting reading to writing. Each chapter has two readings on a related theme. The whole chapter takes approximately 3 hours of class time.

Reading 1 (45 minutes)

1. **Chapter photo and pre-reading questions (5 minutes).** Use the chapter photo and pre-reading questions to introduce the theme of the first reading. Activating students' background knowledge of the topic will make the readings easier to understand.

2. **Activity (10 minutes).** The introductory activity helps students focus on the general theme of the chapter. In Chapter 1, for example, the activity is about other famous artists. In Chapter 2, the activity focuses on general knowledge about English spelling.

3. **Vocabulary and comprehension questions (15 minutes).** To encourage rapid and effective reading skills, you may wish to follow this pattern:

   a. Ask students two or three easy comprehension questions that guide them to the main points of the reading (see the Teaching Hints for suggested focus questions). Set a time limit of about 3 minutes for students to find the answers quickly.

   b. Have students read the Vocabulary questions, work in pairs to answer them, and then go back to the reading to check their answers.

   c. Have students work in pairs to answer the Vocabulary Extension questions and compare their answers as a group.

   d. Have students read the general comprehension questions (Looking for the Main Ideas) and set a time limit of 3 minutes for a second reading of the passage. Then give students 10 minutes to write the answers or discuss them in pairs. Have them check the answers by referring back to the passage.

   e. Give students a chance to search for and guess the meanings of any unknown words. Then ask students to answer the detailed comprehension questions (Skimming and Scanning for Details) and the questions about Making Inferences and Drawing Conclusions, referring back to the passage for the answers.

   f. Use the Teaching Hints for additional ideas on using the reading and extending the comprehension activity.

4. **Discussion (15 minutes).** The discussion questions give students a chance to respond to the readings on a personal level by relating the theme to their concerns and giving their own opinions. The result is a deeper processing of the material, which will help students remember the vocabulary and the theme and develop ideas to use in their writing later. You may assign students to summarize ideas from the discussion for homework.

Reading 2 (90 minutes)

1. **Review (5 minutes).** Review the vocabulary and themes from the first part of the chapter. Extend the vocabulary to include words and phrases related to students' own cultural context, if appropriate. Encourage students to keep a systematic record of new vocabulary in a notebook or on cards, adding definitions and example sentences to help them remember. Check answers to homework, if needed.

2. **Vocabulary and Comprehension questions (15 minutes).** Follow the same procedure as for Reading 1.

3. **Writing (20 minutes or homework, optional).** This writing section emphasizes writing summaries, paraphrasing, and doing research. Familiarize students with the tips on summarizing and paraphrasing at the end of the book. This section is optional, but the research section may help students with writing their essays later in the chapter.

4. **Student essay, follow-up, and exercises (30 minutes).** Use the student essay and follow-up questions to introduce the essay type for the chapter. This section gives students an overview of the essay type and provides language practice specific to this type of essay.

5. **Writing practice (20 minutes).** Get students started on their essay by having them choose a title and brainstorm ideas. Those who work fast can start writing; those who need more time to develop ideas may discuss in pairs or groups.

6. **Video activity or Internet activity (optional).** At the end of each unit, you will find a video activity and an Internet activity. These are all optional and may be used at different stages of the unit, as appropriate. Depending on the theme, you may want to show the video with the first chapter in a unit, for example, or you may want to assign the Internet task as homework and then use it to review the unit in your next lesson.

   a. When you show videos, we recommend that you encourage students to listen and watch for the general meaning only. Play the tapes as often as required for students to be able to complete the task. We do not recommend that you use the video for detailed listening comprehension. The scripts for the videos are provided at the end of this manual.

   b. One of the aims of Internet activities is to provide students with an opportunity to develop the skills needed for independent study. These tasks, therefore, are designed for students to complete on their own time, bringing the results of their research to class for discussion or using the information in their writing. Encourage students to share tips and advice on how to search and to be critical of the information they obtain. Advise students to use a search engine such as **www.google.com** or **www.yahoo.com**. Suggestions for alternative keywords are given in the Teaching Hints. *Note:* Be careful to warn students of the dangers of giving up any personal information to web sites or downloading any files from unknown sources.

7. **Journal homework (optional).** The journal can be used in a variety of ways—as a personal record the student uses for brainstorming ideas; as a dialogue between the teacher and the student; as a class journal, in which each member of the class takes a turn writing his or her opinions and ideas. However you decide to use the journal, you will find many suggestions for journal writing topics in the Teaching Hints.

8. **Assessment (60–80 minutes).** You will find an assessment for each chapter at the end of this manual. The assessment consists of the following:

   a. Ten multiple-choice questions on vocabulary in Reading 1 (20 points)
   b. Ten multiple-choice questions on vocabulary in Reading 2 (20 points)
   c. Ten multiple-choice questions on the grammar or writing skills found in the chapter (30 points)
   d. An essay question (30 points)

(*Note:* Some tests have optional additional writing skills questions.)

The following rubric may be adapted to the needs of your class. Choose the categories you wish to use for your grading. Assign a grade of 1 to 5 for each item (1 = inadequate, 5 = excellent). Add all the grades together and divide by the total number of items in order to find the grade average.

1. **Content**
   a. Clear development of main idea   1 2 3 4 5
   b. Sufficient and relevant supporting details   1 2 3 4 5
   c. Original thinking about the topic   1 2 3 4 5

2. **Organization**
   a. Correct organization of ideas into paragraphs (or within a paragraph)   1 2 3 4 5
   b. Logical sequence of ideas   1 2 3 4 5
   c. Main points and supporting details clearly expressed   1 2 3 4 5

3. **Vocabulary**
   a. Good range of vocabulary for this level   1 2 3 4 5
   b. Appropriate choice of words for this level   1 2 3 4 5

4. **Language use**
   a. Correct use of grammar structures for this level   1 2 3 4 5
   b. Few major errors (in such areas as subject-verb agreement, word order, and tense)   1 2 3 4 5
   c. Correct use of articles, nouns, and prepositions   1 2 3 4 5
   d. Correct use of cohesive devices such as pronouns and transition words   1 2 3 4 5

5. **Mechanics**
   a. Correct spelling and use of punctuation and capitalization   1 2 3 4 5
   b. Correct use of paragraph format   1 2 3 4 5
   c. Good presentation (handwriting is legible; paper is neatly prepared, with title, name, and class)   1 2 3 4 5

Symbol	Explanation
cap	Capital letter
lc	Lowercase (word or words incorrectly capitalized)
p	Punctuation incorrect or missing
sp	Spelling mistake
sv	Mistake in agreement of subject and verb
^	Omission (you have left something out)
frag	Sentence fragment (correct by completing sentence)
ro	Run-on sentence (insert period and capital letter or add comma and conjunction)
vt	Incorrect verb tense
vf	Verb incorrectly formed
modal	Incorrect use or formation of modal
cond	Incorrect use or formation of a conditional sentence
ss	Incorrect sentence structure
wo	Incorrect or awkward word order
conn	Incorrect or missing connector
pass	Incorrect formation or use of passive voice
unclear	Unclear message
art	Incorrect or missing article
num	Problem with the singular or plural of a noun
wc	Wrong word choice, including prepositions
wf	Wrong word form
nonidiom	Nonidiomatic (not expressed this way in English)
coh	Coherence—one idea does not lead to the next
pro re	Pronoun reference unclear or incorrect
pro agree	Pronoun agreement unclear or incorrect
¶	Begin a new paragraph here (indent)

My Friends

vt   I am very lucky to meet many kinds of people in my youthful days. Some

wc   of them only say hi and fleet away. Some of them leave strong impressions on

my mind but soon wave goodbye. However, others stay and become closer and

closer to me as time goes by. Those who choose to stay in my life give me not

only their friendship but also chances to know myself better; that is, I discover

varied aspects of my character through the types of my friends. My friends,

ss   according to their personalities, can be divided into four basic categories: the

romantics, the critics, the philosophers, and the nurturers.

    The romantics are mostly my best friends because we share many

common interests and possess similar qualities. We are spirited in temper

ro   and erratic by nature. We are also incurably sentimental, and unrealistic, the   **p**

most important thing among us is to discuss literary works and write

poems. We skip classes sometimes just because we are not in the right

mood to stay in the classroom and want to go somewhere else. We

understand each other so well that most of the time, by merely a glance, we

immediately catch what the others weep for or laugh at. Being perfectly

matched, we are always envied by other classmates.

    The critics are those I can only admire but rarely have intimate

contact with. We meet mostly in classrooms, club meetings and group

discussions. We have almost nothing in common. However, the reason why we

are friends is because I want someone to teach and analyze the real world

for me, and they happen to need someone to listen to their opinions. In

class, they are talkative, active and are often the ones who are eager to

have debate. They focus all their attention to instructors' lectures to the   **wc**

point of trying to find fault in them. Though I don't quite agree to their   **wc**

"aggressive" manner, I must admit that they are really somebody. I like to

watch them in some distance so as not to be involved in their argument.   **wc**

modal	Also, such a distance could allow me to appreciate with ease their outstanding skills of observing and criticizing.
lc	The Philosophers are often thought to be strange, because they are unsocial, pensive, and self-indulgent. Yet for me, they are like hidden treasures, waiting for the right time to be explored. We spend most of our time in silence, reading or contemplating. Though it sometimes seems boring to be with them, it is worthwhile. They dare to overturn old concepts and always burst out something intelligent and inspiring. They like to sit behind **wc** the classroom, burying their heads in books or looking out of the window. I
cond	would not disturb them; rather, I would stare at them as if they were greek **cap** statues. They are rarely associated with emotions, for they all wear a serious facial expression. However, once something touches their hearts,
cond	they would cry louder than anyone. I cherish their boldness of their thoughts **art** and frailty of their feelings.
	If the friendship with the romantics is built upon passion, then with the nurturers it is upon tenderness. The nurturers are soft, kind, considerate, and forbearing. Though with them I can hardly share my
num	fantasies, they are the very persons I would turn to every time I need hearty comfort. When I am sick, they pass me hot water, tissues, and encouraging
cond	notes. When they find me distracted in class, they would tap my shoulder to warn me. However, they usually have serious homesick. They manage to go **nonidiom** home at least twice a month. When they go back to school, they have to
art	spend few days recovering form sadness. Their family is always their favorite **sp**
wc	subject. There's no exaggeration that at the moment I know them, I know their **pro re** moms as well! Possessing both tenderness of a mother and dependence of a **art** child, these nurturers are remarkably cute and attracting.
pro agree	Each kind of my friends has their own unique personalities. The **num**
wf	romantics are sentimental, the critics are argumental, the philosophers are pensive, and the nurturers are tender. Though I am more attached to the romantics and the nurturers, I appreciate and cherish the critics and the philosophers. They together meet my different needs and enrich my life.

Unit One	Symbols

Chapter One

Color Me Pink

Audio CD, Track 1

Teaching Hints

The readings and activities in this unit describe some hidden meanings associated with certain colors and numbers. Some of our beliefs about colors and numbers are thousands of years old. Here are some interesting facts about colors:

- The room where people wait before appearing on TV shows is usually painted green because studies have shown that the color green helps people feel calm and relaxed.
- Yellow is the hardest color for the eye to take in, and babies have been found to cry more in rooms painted yellow.
- Pink has been shown to tranquilize people. Sports teams sometimes paint the locker room used by the opposing team pink so that the team will lose energy.

Warm-up   You may start the lesson in one of these ways:

- Have students look at the symbols on the unit opener page. The symbol on the left—a rod entwined by a snake, with the "star of life" in the background—signifies emergency medicine. It comes from the magic rod of Hermes, the Greek messenger of the gods. The symbol on the top right tells that facilities for disabled persons are available. The third symbol signifies peace. Have students think of some symbols that are used in their country. Then ask students to define the word *symbol*. (It's something that expresses an idea without using words.)
- Ask students to stand up and form groups according to the main color of the clothing they are wearing that day. Point out different parts of the room where those wearing mostly green, blue, pink, etc., can gather. Ask the students to discuss among themselves how the color they are wearing makes them feel. After a few minutes, invite the groups to share their findings with the class.
- Write the following color names on the board: black, white, green, yellow. Ask different students to tell the class about any special significance each color has for people in their culture or for them personally. Compare the meanings each color has for different cultural groups and individuals.

Reading   Ask students to read the first sentence of each paragraph to get a general understanding of the reading passage. Then ask such questions as

Which paragraph tells us about colorgenics? (paragraph 3)
Which paragraphs discuss how colors affect us? (paragraphs 6 and 7)

Then write the following questions on the board and ask students to read the entire passage:

What do the colors we wear communicate to others?
What does the word *colorgenics* mean?
What color is helpful in treating depression? Heart disease?

When students finish reading, discuss the questions with the class. During the discussion, ask students to point out the section of the reading passage that answers each question.

Journal   Write about your favorite color. When did you first discover it was your favorite color? How does it make you feel? How do you make use of that color in your life?

Chapter One Answer Key

Predicting, p. 2
1. e   2. a   3. f   4. d   5. c   6. b

Vocabulary
Meaning, p. 5
1. ailments   2. soothe   3. stimulating   4. subconsciously
5. coincidence   6. attitude   7. contentment   8. Pace

Word Building, p. 5
1. a. symbolizes b. symbolically   2. a. emotionally b. emotions
3. a. psychologists b. psychological

Comprehension
Looking for the Main Ideas, p. 6
1. c   2. c   3. a

Looking for Details, p. 7
1. A person who likes to wear pink is warm and understanding.
2. White symbolizes purity in many cultures.
3. Yellow is a symbol of luck in Peru.
4. Red makes us feel stimulated and excited.
5. Blue makes us feel calm.
6. Green is good for heart conditions.
7. The Luscher color test is used to help psychologists' patients.

Making Inferences and Drawing Conclusions, p. 8
Possible answers:
1. A decorator could choose colors that would help people feel calm and happy in their homes.
2. Colors have strong symbolic meanings.
3. The psychologist could find out about patients' personalities, based on the colors they like and dislike.
4. We could learn to use color to make ourselves and others happier.
5. I would use soft blue in a child's bedroom because it is a calming color and bright yellow in a classroom because it energizes people.

Writing
Exercise 1, p. 10

Topic	Controlling Idea
1. The colors we wear	change our emotions
2. People who wear orange	like to communicate with others
3. People who wear red clothes	want to have fun
4. Shoes	give us lots of information about the person wearing them
5. Patterns on clothing	give us clues to the mood of the wearer
6. People who wear yellow	are often creative
7. Turquoise	is good for people who have decisions to make
8. People who wear green	often like the outdoors

Exercise 2, p. 10
1. c   2. a   3. a   4. c

Exercise 3, p. 12
Possible answers:
1. A person's favorite color reveals something about his or her personality.
2. Colors can have positive effects on health.
3. A color wheel can help you identify your favorite colors and their healing aspects.

Chapter One Assessment Answer Key

Vocabulary
1. b   2. c   3. d   4. a   5. b   6. c   7. b   8. b   9. c   10. d

Grammar/Language
1. c   2. a   3. c   4. b   5. b   6. c   7. d   8. a   9. c   10. c

Chapter Two

And the Lucky Number Is . . .   Audio CD, Track 2

Teaching Hints

Here are some interesting superstitions:

* Breaking a mirror brings seven years of bad luck.
* If a broken clock suddenly starts working, someone in the house will die.
* If you say goodbye to a friend on a bridge, you will never see that person again.

Warm-up   You may start the lesson in one of these ways:

* Ask students to share with the class some superstitions they pay attention to, even though they may not really believe in them. For example, they may avoid walking under a ladder even though they don't think it will necessarily bring bad luck. Start off the discussion with superstitions you believe in.
* If there are students from several different cultures in your class, invite them to tell about animal or number superstitions that are found in their part of

the world. If possible, compare and contrast superstitions about a particular animal or number across several different cultures.

- Ask each student to write his or her own lucky number on a slip of paper. Then put the numbers in a box, and have a class lottery. Choose two or three winners. (You may wish to give the winners a small prize, such as a candy bar.) Have the winners tell why they consider the number they wrote down to be their lucky number.

Using the Photo   Discuss the symbols in the photos. (Having a black cat cross your path is unlucky, as is Friday the 13th. Finding a four-leafed clover is lucky.) Ask students what other animal, plant, or number superstitions they know of.

Pre-Reading Activity   Ask students what superstitions they have heard of in connection with numbers. List their responses on the board. As students read the passage, ask them to note how many of the superstitions listed on the board are mentioned in it.

Journal   Interview older family members and friends about lucky numbers and other superstitions they believe in. Describe the superstitions. Tell how each person came to adopt this particular belief. What proof or examples does he or she give to support the belief that the superstition is true?

Culture Cue   Remind students that, although they may not believe in a particular superstition, it may have deep significance to a person from another culture. It is important to be sensitive to the feelings of others who have belief systems different from our own.

CNN.com.

Video Activity   Brainstorm a list of possible uses for materials that can change their color: plastic, metal, and fabric. Make a cluster diagram on the board. Compare these ideas with those in the video. Review the questions before watching the video. (See the video script on page 167.)

Internet Activity   If students are interested, suggest that they research the numbers of a famous person's birthdate along with their own. Suggested keywords: *numerology, lucky numbers, number superstitions, lucky dates.*

Chapter Two Answer Key

Vocabulary
Meaning, p. 16
1. a   2. a   3. b   4. b   5. d   6. a   7. d

Word Building, p. 17
1. a. superstitious   b. superstitions   2. a. lucky   b. luck
3. a. believe   b. belief

Comprehension
Looking for the Main Ideas, p. 18
1. b   2. a   3. d

Looking for Details, p. 18
1. A seventh child had special gifts.
2. A dream repeated three times will come true.
3. The seventh year in a person's life brought great change.
4. Three was lucky because it symbolized birth, life, and death.
5. Five is considered a holy and lucky number in Egypt.
6. Four symbolized unity, endurance, and balance.
7. One of the earliest written stories about the number 13 appeared in Norwegian mythology.
8. The thirteenth day of the month is considered unlucky for new enterprises or journeys.
9. They give a room the number 12A or 14 instead of 13.

Making Inferences and Drawing Conclusions, p. 20
Possible answers:
1. Pythagoras stated that things happen in sets of three.
2. A seventh child might be thought of as special because the number seven was thought to govern the lives of human beings.
3. People might not want to stay in a room with the number 13 on it.
4. Belief in the power of numbers has persisted in spite of the advances made by science and technology.
5. People believe in superstitions because they are a way of making the world feel safer and more controllable.

Writing
Exercise 1, p. 24
The thesis statements are items 1, 4, 6, 8, 10.

Exercise 2, p. 26
Possible answers:
I. Introduction
   Thesis statement: Two of the most popular superstitions are concerned with the evil eye and throwing water.
II. Body
   A. Topic sentence: People believe that they must protect themselves . . . .
      1. Support: second sentence in paragraph
      2. Support: third sentence in paragraph
      3. Support: fourth sentence in paragraph
   B. Topic sentence: Another popular superstition . . . .
      1. Support: second sentence in paragraph
      2. Support: fourth sentence in paragraph
      3. Support: fifth sentence in paragraph

Do you know these symbols? p. 27
1. b   2. a   3. c   4. b   5. b   6. a   7. b

Video Activity, p. 28
ultraviolet (UV) (adjective): relating to certain invisible rays of light
to expose (verb): to uncover or show
a pigment (noun): a substance (like the powder shown in the video) used in dyes to give color to cloth or other material
application (noun): use

1. The video shows that changing colors can be used in toys, clothing, cars, and plastics, and they may be used in credit cards and money in the future.

2. a. False (light, not heat)   b. False (from blue to white)
c. food   d. photochromic colors have many uses

3. Possible answers:

a. Some people would enjoy wearing clothes with photochromic colors just for fun and variety.

b. Color changes might affect people's moods.

c. Cheerful or soothing colors might help heal people.

Chapter Two Assessment Answer Key

Vocabulary
1. a   2. d   3. c   4. b   5. b   6. b   7. d   8. c   9. b   10. a

Grammar/Language
1. T   2. F   3. T   4. T   5. T   6. F   7. T   8. T   9. T   10. T

Chapter Three

An American Holiday, Hawaiian Style

Audio CD, Track 3

Teaching Hints

The readings and activities in Chapter Three focus on some interesting holiday and festival customs in Hawaii and China. Chapter Four presents information about some other holidays and describes a frog jumping contest that has become a California tradition. Here are some interesting facts about customs around the world:

- As part of the New Year celebration in Ecuador, families burn a toy figure outside their house. The destruction of the toy figure represents getting rid of anything bad that happened during the previous year.
- In Denmark, people save old dishes all year long and throw them at their friends' houses on New Year's Eve. Many broken dishes show that a family has a lot of friends.

Warm-up   You may start the lesson in one of these ways:

- Describe the clothing of the women in the photo on the unit opener page. What do students think of dressing in traditional clothes? Ask them to draw or describe clothes from their own cultures and traditions.
- Ask each student to name her or his favorite holiday food. Group the students according to their choices. Have the groups discuss the different ways this food can be prepared and present their results to the class.
- Have students make a list of facts they know about Hawaii. Compare lists and see if there are contradictions. Then have students write three questions about things they would like to know about Hawaii. If no one in the class can answer these questions, assign them as a homework task.

Reading   To help students get a general idea of the information in the reading passage, ask them to read the first sentence in each paragraph. Then ask:

Which paragraphs describe holiday celebrations in U.S. states other than Hawaii? (paragraphs 1 and 2)
Which paragraphs describe the preparation of Thanksgiving food in Hawaii? (paragraphs 4, 5, 6, 7, 8, and 9)

Extension Activity   More advanced students may benefit from doing a summarizing activity. Ask them to take notes as they listen to the audio or reread the text. Then have them present an oral summary to the class.

Journal   Write about a recent holiday celebration with your family. Name the holiday, explain its significance, and describe what you did, what you wore, and what you ate. Tell whether you enjoyed it or not.

Chapter Three Answer Key

Vocabulary
Meaning, p. 32
1. piled up   2. pasted   3. trace   4. patted down   5. line   6. emerge
7. shovel   8. Bundles

Word Building, p. 33
1. a. celebrate b. celebration   2. a. Traditional b. tradition
3. a. carefully b. careful

Comprehension
Looking for the Main Ideas, p. 33
1. b   2. c   3. d

Looking for Details, p. 34
1. luau   2. an imu   3. collect stones   4. line the hole with stones
5. several rocks are put inside the turkey or pig
6. pieces of the banana plant, ti leaves, bundles of food
7. ti leaves, wet sacks, a canvas covering   8. Three or four

Making Inferences and Drawing Conclusions, p. 35
Possible answers:
1. The people in different parts of the United States have different ethnic backgrounds.
2. It is an island. It is the only state in the United States that was once an independent nation with its own language and culture.
3. Holidays are a time when people honor their historical roots.
4. Both parents and children get involved.
5. The dirt holds in the heat while the food cooks.

Writing
Model Essay, p. 36
Thesis statement: First sentence in paragraph 1
Paragraph 2 topic sentence: first sentence in paragraph
Paragraph 3 topic sentence: first sentence in paragraph
Paragraph 4 topic sentence: first sentence in paragraph
Paragraph 5 topic sentence: first sentence in paragraph

Chronological Order, p. 37
Paragraph 5: before
Paragraph 6: first, then, finally, then, then
Paragraph 7: before, finally
Paragraph 8: then
Paragraph 9: later, then

Exercise 1, p. 38
Introduction 1: 3, 2, 4, 1
Introduction 2: 1, 3, 4, 2, 5
Introduction 3: 2, 1, 5, 3, 4
Introduction 4: 3, 1, 4, 5, 2

Chapter Three Assessment Answer Key

Vocabulary
1. c   2. b   3. c   4. a   5. d   6. b   7. a   8. c   9. b   10. a

Grammar/Language
1. b   2. b   3. c   4. a   5. c   6. c   7. d   8. a   9. c   10. d

Chapter Four

Hop to It!

Audio CD, Track 4

Teaching Hints

Here are some interesting facts about Mark Twain (1835–1910) and his story "The Celebrated Jumping Frog of Calaveras County."

- Mark Twain grew up in Hannibal, Missouri. His real name was Samuel Langhorne Clemens; the name Mark Twain came from the words used by riverboat captains as they measured the depth of the river bottom. At various times in his life, he worked as a printer, a writer, and a riverboat pilot. He traveled widely and wrote about what he saw, usually in a humorous way.
- Twain's story "The Celebrated Jumping Frog of Calaveras County" made him famous. It was first published in 1865, when Twain was a struggling journalist in California, and it inspired a contest that is still held today. The Calaveras County Fair and Jumping Frog Contest is held the third weekend of each year at the Calaveras County Fairgrounds, better known as Frogtown.

Warm-up   You may start the lesson in one of these ways:

- Ask students to share experiences they have had in trying to train pets. Invite them to tell what they wanted to teach the animal to do and how successful they were.
- Bring to class photos of animal competitions, such as a horse race, a dressage competition, and a dog obedience show. Divide the class into groups, and give each group a picture to discuss. Have one person from each group show the picture to the rest of the class and summarize the group's discussion.
- Bring in photos of different animals—lions, elephants, horses, dogs, goats, cats, monkeys, parrots, fish—and discuss whether or not each animal can easily be trained to help humans.

Reading   To help students get a general idea of the information in the reading passage, ask them to read the first and the last paragraphs. Then ask:

How old is this frog jumping contest?
How many people attended it at first?
How many people attend it now?
What activities have been added over the years?

Play the audio or read the passage aloud to help students find the answers to these questions.

Additional Discussion Questions

Why do you think humans are so interested in training animals?
Do you think animals understand what they are doing when they perform tricks?
Do you think it is cruel to train animals for human entertainment?

Journal   For a week, note in your journal all of the animals you encounter in the street or on television or at the movies. Describe each animal, tell where you saw it, and report what it was doing.

Culture Cue   Some people believe that it is cruel for humans to train animals. Some cultures have taboos about touching certain types of animals or keeping them as pets.

CNN.com   **Video Activity**   Have students make a list of all the different ways in which they think seafood might be cooked in New England. Review the questions and the vocabulary before watching the video. (See the video script on page 167.)

Internet Activity   You might suggest that students compare customs relating to a specific event in various societies. For example, how are marriage customs different in different countries? Suggested keywords: the name of the custom (for example, *marriage customs*) followed by the name of a country (for example, *India*)

Chapter Four Answer Key

Vocabulary
Meaning, p. 42
1. a   2. d   3. a   4. b   5. a   6. a   7. b   8. b   9. d   10. d

Word Building, p. 43
1. a. competitors b. competitive   2. a. entry b. entrants
3. a. predict b. predictable

Comprehension
Looking for the Main Ideas, p. 44
1. c   2. a   3. d

Looking for Details, p. 45
1. The idea for the Jumping Frog Contest came from a short story by Mark Twain.
2. The contest takes place each year.
3. Approximately 50,000 people attend the contest.
4. The entry fee includes the cost of renting a frog.
5. People can rent a frog.
6. The "jockey" tries to make the frog jump.
7. The frog must make three jumps.
8. The frogs lift weights, eat centipede soup, and do high dives.

Making Inferences and Drawing Conclusions, p. 46
Possible answers:
1. People enjoy simple, uncomplicated ways of having fun.
2. The sponsors make their money from the food, rides, and other attractions.
3. The "jockey" wants his or her frog to move ahead, not backwards.
4. Frogs can't really be trained.
5. They enjoy the contest whether or not they win.

Writing
Exercise 1, p. 48
Possible answers:
Conclusion 2: In summary, Japan's elaborate rules for table manners have a long tradition.
Conclusion 3: In summary, birthday celebrations, though different around the world, have the same purpose: to symbolically celebrate a person's life.

Do you know these customs? p. 49
1. T   2. T   3. F (This is done only when you wish to have your coffee cup fortune read.)   4. F (This is a custom in many Middle Eastern countries.)
5. T   6. F (This custom started in Germany in the 1700s.)

Video Activity, p. 49
2. The following foods are shown in the video: onions, clams, potatoes, lobster, and clam chowder. (Corn on the cob and mussels are also shown.)
3. The correct order is (1) dig a pit, (2) set down rocks, (3) heat the rocks with a fire, and (4) add the clams. (There are several layers of rocks and clams.)

Chapter Four Assessment Answer Key

Vocabulary
1. c   2. a   3. b   4. c   5. a   6. b   7. b   8. c   9. b   10. a

Grammar/Language
1. T   2. T   3. F   4. F   5. T   6. T   7. T   8. F   9. T   10. F

3 · HINTS/KEY

| Chapter Five | **Bumps and Personalities** | Audio CD, Track 5 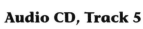 |

Teaching Hints

The readings and follow-up activities in this unit focus on the interconnections among body, mind, and personality. Chapter Five suggests how a person's physical form may reveal personality characteristics. Chapter Six looks at medical therapies that treat the whole person, not just a single physical complaint. Here are some interesting facts about phrenology, the study of bumps on the head:

- Although phrenology is not regarded as a science, it provided an important first step toward modern medical research into how different areas within the brain function.
- During the nineteenth century, some people studied phrenology in an attempt to find compatible marriage partners.

Warm-up

You may start the lesson in one of these ways:

- Ask students to describe what the person in the photo on page 51 is doing. Invite anyone who knows to explain what tai chi is. (The person practices a set of physical movements that look like ballet while concentrating the mind deeply on the process. Regular practice of tai chi is said to boost the immune system, decrease anxiety and depression, and reduce asthma and allergy problems.)
- Bring in photos of different film stars or personalities. Number them, and put them up on the walls of your classroom. Have students walk around and identify each number with a personality trait. Then compare results on the board.

Reading

Before the first reading, write the words *physiognomy* and *phrenology* on the board. Divide the class into two groups, and ask one group to read the second paragraph about physiognomy and the other to read the fourth paragraph about phrenology. Then call on students from the two groups to explain what the terms mean. Make notes on the board. Then read and discuss the comprehension questions on page 56 and have students read the text on their own, looking for the answers.

Pronunciation

Play the audio or read the passage aloud so that students can hear the pronunciation of any difficult vocabulary. You may wish to have students raise their hand whenever they hear a difficult word so that you can pause and practice the word together.

Journal

Choose a picture of a person from a newspaper or magazine, and write a short description of the person's personality, based on her or his appearance.

Culture Cue

Be careful to avoid referring to the facial characteristics of students in your class or generalizing about appearance based on ethnicity.

Chapter Five Answer Key

Predicting, p. 52
1. not answered in text   2. e   3. d   4. b   5. a

Vocabulary
Meaning, p. 54
1. a   2. c   3. b   4. b   5. c   6. b   7. a   8. d   9. b

Word Building, p. 55
1. a. decisive b. decisions   2. a. courageous b. courage
3. a. scientists b. scientific

Comprehension
Looking for the Main Ideas, p. 56
1. c   2. d   3. a

Looking for Details, p. 57
1. F   2. T   3. F   4. F   5. F   6. T   7. F   8. F   9. F

Making Inferences and Drawing Conclusions, p. 57
Possible answers:
1. They wanted to understand human behavior better.
2. He was looking for a scientific way of explaining personality.
3. They didn't believe his theory.
4. Other doctors ridiculed him, and he couldn't get a good job.
5. A physiognomist might say that the person is not practical and does not think clearly, because those physical characteristics indicate curiosity, indecisiveness, and an artistic nature.

Writing
Model Essay, p. 61
Thesis statement: last sentence in paragraph 1
Paragraph 2 topic sentence: first sentence in paragraph
Paragraph 3 topic sentence: first sentence in paragraph
Paragraph 4 topic sentence: first sentence in paragraph
Paragraph 5 topic sentence: first sentence in paragraph

The Example Essay, p. 63
Paragraph 2: one example, for example, also, also, e.g.
Paragraph 3: another example, also
Paragraph 4: finally, also, for instance

Exercise 1, p. 64
for example, For instance, for example

Chapter Five Assessment Answer Key

Vocabulary
1. a   2. b   3. c   4. d   5. c   6. b   7. c   8. c   9. b   10. a

Grammar/Language
1. d   2. b   3. c   4. a   5. d   6. a   7. b   8. c   9. c   10. d

Chapter Six

The Many Faces of Medicine   Audio CD, Track 6

Teaching Hints

Here are some interesting facts about alternative medicine:

- Energy therapy is based on the theory that an important component of the human body is its energy field. Blockages in this force field, which surrounds the body, are thought to produce stress, anxiety, and physical illness. Practices such as yoga and chiropractic adjustment are used to help the energy flow freely so that health can be restored.
- Acupuncture, the use of needles carefully placed in various parts of the body to relieve pain, is an ancient Chinese remedy. It may have been discovered during the process of tattooing. Acupuncture is so well accepted in Western countries today that many health insurance companies reimburse patients for acupuncture treatments.

Warm-up   You may start the lesson in one of these ways:

- Ask students to form groups to research one of the following types of alternative medicine: reflexology, homeopathy, or aromatherapy. Then ask students to describe to the class the alternative medical treatment their group studied and bring in any advertisements, brochures, or pictures they can find to illustrate their topic.
- On the board, make a chart of common ailments (headache, backache, upset stomach, etc.). Ask students to tell how doctors usually treat each problem. Then brainstorm with the class some possible alternative treatments, such as herbal medicine and chiropractic care.
- Invite students to describe any personal experiences they have had with complementary or alternative medical treatments. Ask them to tell about the treatment and say whether or not they felt it was effective.

Reading   After completing the pre-reading and predicting activities on page 67, draw a two-column chart on the board with these headings: *Western Scientific Medicine* and *Alternative Medicine*. Ask students to copy the chart and then, as they do the reading, list examples in each column. After they finish reading, review the lists with the class. You may also do this activity while listening to the audio.

Alternative Reading Activity   Ask more advanced students to read the passage only once and not look back as they answer the follow-up questions. If you want to make the activity even more challenging, set a time limit for the reading.

Journal   Describe how you feel at various hours of the day. What activities or treatments might make you feel better at your low points during the day?

CNN.com.   Video Activity   Review anything that students already know about yoga. Then make a list of questions about yoga that students would like to have answered. Review the questions and the vocabulary before watching the video. (See the video script on page 168.)

Internet Activity Instead of having the whole class research phrenology, you might wish to have some students look up information on alternative therapies such as reflexology, homeopathy, and aromatherapy.

Chapter Six Answer Key

Vocabulary
Meaning, p. 69
1. b   2. b   3. d   4. a   5. d   6. a   7. c   8. b   9. a   10. a

Word Building, p. 71
1. a. effects b. effective   2. a. successful b. successfully   3 a. proof b. prove

Comprehension
Looking for the Main Ideas, p. 71
1. a   2. c   3. c

Looking for Details, p. 72
1. Holistic doctors believe that the parts of the body are interconnected and must be treated as a whole.
2. Acupuncture and hypnotism are two examples of the use of alternative medicine.
3. Acupuncture and biofeedback are highly respected forms of alternative medicine.
4. We do not have proof that reflexology works.
5. African herbalists use tree bark, roots, and grasses to make medicine.
6. The Chinese have been practicing acupuncture for approximately 2,000 years.
7. Five treatments being studied are meditation, homeopathy, chiropractic medicine, biofeedback, and herbal medicine.
8. With biofeedback, a person learns to recognize and control muscle tension and blood pressure.

Making Inferences and Drawing Conclusions, p. 73
Possible answers:
1. Conventional medicine may not have cured them.
2. They have gained prestige because scientific experiments have shown that some of them are effective.
3. The doctor might prescribe meditation to calm the nerves.
4. Some forms of alternative medicine have been researched more thoroughly than others.
5. Conventional doctors have spent years learning about drugs and surgery and don't understand alternative medicine.

Writing
Exercise 1, p. 75
2. African herbalists use parts of a tree, such as the bark, to make teas.
3. Some forms of alternative medicine, such as the practice of acupuncture, are highly respected.
4. Researchers today can choose from among many forms of alternative medicine, such as herbal medicine, homeopathy, and chiropractic medicine.
5. Some practices, such as reflexology, feel good, but there is little proof that they work.
6. Homeopathy helps patients with problems such as headaches and allergies.

Exercise 2, p. 76
1. Homeopathy, for instance, . . .
2. Biofeedback is successful in treating the following: . . .
3. For instance, . . .
4. No punctuation necessary.
5. As an example, . . .
6. In some European countries, e.g., France, . . .

Do you know these facts about your body? p. 79
1. b   2. a   3. c   4. a   5. c   6. b

Video Activity, p. 80
1. Possible answer: Yoga is a system of exercises based on Hindu philosophy. Yoga exercises help quiet the body and concentrate the mind.
2. a. 10 million b. gentle poses, breathing, meditation c. carpal tunnel syndrome, diabetes, arthritis d. reduced stress and improved concentration
3. Possible tips: Find a good yoga instructor; start slowly; avoid certain poses if you have back pain or other health problems.

Chapter Six Assessment Answer Key

Vocabulary
1. c   2. b   3. c   4. a   5. a   6. d   7. d   8. c   9. d   10. a

Grammar/Language
1. T   2. F   3. F   4. T   5. F   6. T   7. F   8. T   9. T   10. T

| Chapter Seven | **The Shakers** | Audio CD, Track 7 |

Teaching Hints

This unit focuses on the lives of extraordinary people. Chapter Seven describes the Shakers, a group formed in the eighteenth century by people who wanted to live communally and didn't believe in marriage. Chapter Eight summarizes the accomplishments of George Washington Carver, an African American who became famous for discovering 100 uses for peanuts. Here are some interesting facts about the Shakers:

- Shaker villages have been made into museums in several different states across the United States, including Massachusetts, New Hampshire, New York, and Ohio.
- Rather than dying out, the Shaker community in Sabbath Day Lake, Maine, is beginning to expand.

Warm-up   You may start the lesson in one of these ways:

- Ask students to look at the unit opener photo on page 81 and say what they think is happening. Accept all reasonable responses. Point out that whatever is happening involves the careful cooperation of a large group and is attracting the attention of many more people. Explain that the people described in this unit place a high value on teamwork and have received a lot of attention for their accomplishments. (The picture was taken at the Casteller Festival in Barcelona, Spain. Casteller groups come from all around the region to build human towers during this festival.)
- Display pictures of the following items or bring in the actual objects: a broom, a clothespin, a package of garden seeds. Ask what people did before these items were invented. (They used inefficient circular brooms. They draped clothes over the line without pins, and the clothes often blew off. They kept seeds in cans or bottles.) Explain that these are inventions of the Shakers, a group of people whom students will read about in Chapter Seven.

Extension Activity   After going over the vocabulary and comprehension questions with the class, play the audio or read the passage aloud and have students write down all the adjectives they hear. Then have them explain how each adjective is related to the topic.

Journal   Write about beliefs, practices, daily life, and special accomplishments of the people in a community that you are familiar with. If possible, write about a group from your native country.

Chapter Seven Answer Key

Vocabulary
Meaning, p. 84
1. b   2. a   3. c   4. a   5. a   6. b   7. c   8. a   9. b   10. d

Word Building, p. 86
1. a. creative b. created   2. a. kindness b. kind
3. a. inventive b. inventions

Comprehension
Looking for the Main Ideas, p. 87
1. b   2. d   3. a

Looking for Details, p. 87
1. Ann Lee brought the Shakers to America.
2. The Shakers admired kindness, generosity, modesty, purity, and cleanliness.
3. A man and a woman could have a conversation together with others present.
4. A Shaker man wore dark pants and a simple coat.
5. The Shakers invented a revolving oven, a washing machine, and a wood-burning stove.
6. The Shakers walked in the woods and took carriage rides.

Making Inferences and Drawing Conclusions, p. 88
Possible answers:
1. The man and woman would live separately, and the child would live with the parent of the same sex.
2. They wanted a more peaceful way of life.
3. They weren't distracted by worldly concerns.
4. They didn't want to have to depend on people who didn't share their beliefs.
5. They wanted to make it easier for men and women not to be attracted to each other.

Writing
Model Essay, p. 90
Thesis statement: last sentence in paragraph 1
Paragraph 2 topic sentence: first sentence in paragraph
Paragraph 3 topic sentence: first sentence in paragraph
Paragraph 4 topic sentence: first sentence in paragraph

The Dominant Impression, p. 91
Paragraph 1: a teacher, very nice person, very good qualities
Paragraph 2: believes all people are equal
Paragraph 3: a good leader
Paragraph 4: very nice, a very good teacher, the best company

Exercise 1, p. 91
1. a, e   2. b, c, d   3. b, c

Chapter Seven Assessment Answer Key

Vocabulary
1. c   2. a   3. c   4. b   5. d   6. a   7. a   8. c   9. b   10. c

Grammar/Language

1. b   2. d   3. c   4. a   5. d   6. d   7. b   8. c   9. a   10. c

Chapter Eight

George Washington Carver   Audio CD, Track 8

Teaching Hints

Warm-up   You may start the lesson in one of these ways:

- With students, brainstorm a list of famous African Americans and their achievements. The list might include the following pioneers in the American civil rights movement: Harriet Tubman (1820–1913); Martin Luther King, Jr. (1929–1968); Rosa Parks (born 1913).
- Elicit from students what they know about the history of civil rights in America, and have them research famous dates and achievements of African Americans.

Reading   After discussing the pre-reading questions in the book, write these questions on the board:

   What was Carver's early life like?
   How was Carver able to attend college?
   Why did peanuts become so important to Southern farmers?

Then have students read the story, looking for the answers to these three questions.

Extension Activity   After they have read and answered the vocabulary and comprehension questions, have students listen to the audio and, as they listen, note down all the numbers they hear (1861; 1865; 12; 12; 1890; 1891; 1896; 300; 1921; 100; 1930; 100,000; 125; 1940; 33,000; 1943). Then have students work in pairs to remember what each number meant in the story.

Journal   Write a brief description of how a minority group is (or was) treated in your home country. Name the group, describe who the members are, tell where they came from, and tell how they are (or were) treated differently from other citizens.

Culture Cue   Some of the material in this chapter could arouse painful feelings among students who have experienced discrimination because of their minority status. Be sure to take this into account as you monitor class discussions.

CNN.com   Video Activity   Discuss briefly the influence that photography has had on our society and our ideas about art. Do any of the students take photographs? Where and when? What do they take pictures of? What do they like about taking pictures? Go over the questions and the vocabulary before watching the video. (See the video script on page 169.)

 Internet Activity   You might ask students to write a short summary of what they find out about Shakers and download a picture of some Shaker people or Shaker products. Have them display their writing and pictures in the classroom so that others can look at them.

Chapter Eight Answer Key

Vocabulary
Meaning, p. 96
1. b   2. d   3. a   4. a   5. c   6. a
7. d   8. b   9. c   10. a   11. b

Word Building, p. 98
1. a. worn b. wear   2. a. discovered b. discoveries
3. a. Agricultural b. agriculture

Comprehension
Looking for the Main Ideas, p. 98
1. a   2. b   3. d

Looking for Details, p. 99
1. F   2. T   3. T   4. T   5. F   6. F   7. F

Making Inferences and Drawing Conclusions, p. 99
Possible answers:
1. They were kind and generous.
2. He was trying to get an education.
3. Black Americans were not allowed to attend some schools.
4. Booker T. Washington had heard of the important agricultural research that George Washington Carver had done.
5. He wanted to support a school that black Americans attended.
6. Many farmers switched from cotton to peanuts.

Writing, p. 101
Paragraph 2: soon after, in 1865, at age 12
Paragraph 3: for the next 12 years, when, eventually, in 1890, soon
Paragraph 4: in 1891, after
Paragraph 5: one day
Paragraph 6: in 1896, after a while, now
Paragraph 7: meanwhile
Paragraph 8: by the 1930s
Paragraph 9: in 1940, in 1943

Exercise 1, p. 101
3, 1, 5, 8, 2, 4, 7, 10, 11, 13, 6, 9, 12

Exercise 2, p. 103
Paragraph 1: greatest scientists, quiet . . . kind man, he . . . rich, greatest good, greatest number
Paragraph 2: last name
Paragraph 3: next . . . years, he . . . black
Paragraph 4: black student, small jobs, special work, work . . . outstanding
Paragraph 5: respected black educator, black agricultural school, poor black school, high salary
Paragraph 6: new ways; poor, struggling farmers; different crops, soil . . . richer, more peanuts, more money
Paragraph 7: many uses, more uses, peanut man, many prizes . . . awards, more products, postage stamps
Paragraph 8: Carver . . . famous, generous offer, monthly salary
Paragraph 9: life savings, golden door

Do you know who they are? p. 105

1. F (The first woman in space was a Russian—Valentina Tereshkova in 1963. Sally Ride was the first U.S. woman astronaut; she rode aboard the Challenger in 1983.)
2. T
3. F (They originally came from India, where they belonged to a caste called the Dom; 1,000 years ago, the Dom started to move west out of India.)
4. T
5. F (It was Jacques Cousteau.)
6. T

Video Activity, p. 105

1. Austin Hansen took photos of politicians and other influential figures (Malcolm X; Adam Clayton Powell, Jr.; Emperor Haile Selassie of Ethiopia; the Queen Mother of England; educator Mary McLeod Bethune; Martin Luther King, Jr.; New York Mayor David Dinkins); photos of buildings (he served as historian for a number of Harlem churches); news photos of ordinary people (a crowd reading about the death of Franklin Delano Roosevelt, a woman and her baby who had just been evicted from their home); photos of musicians (jazz pianist Count Basie, singer Eartha Kitt, jazz trumpeter Dizzy Gillespie); and war photos (during World War II, he served as a Navy photographer's mate). He took photos of sports personalities, (baseball greats Roy Campanella and Jackie Robinson at a Boys' Club), but *not* sports events.
2. a. the Virgin Islands b. 1928 c. drums d. historian

Chapter Eight Assessment Answer Key

Vocabulary
1. a   2. d   3. c   4. d   5. b   6. a   7. c   8. b   9. b   10. c

Grammar/Language
1. b   2. a   3. d   4. c   5. b   6. a   7. d   8. c   9. b   10. a

Chapter Nine   **A Variety of American Foods**   **Audio CD, Track 9**

Teaching Hints

This unit describes eating and drinking habits that have developed in various parts of the world. Chapter Nine focuses on the kinds of foods that are prevalent in different parts of the United States. Chapter Ten describes the wide variety of teas and tea-drinking customs found in different countries. Here are some interesting facts about food in the United States:

- People in the southern part of the United States enjoy drinking iced tea with meals, even in the winter. They drink it with lemon and lots of sugar.
- People who live in Maine, the northeastern-most state in the United States, are known for their delicious lobster picnics. The most authentic way to cook lobster is to boil this sea creature in sea water over a wood fire on an ocean beach.
- Sushi is a typical food from Japan, made from rice, seaweed, and raw fish. It has been adapted for U.S. tastes into the now-famous California roll—sushi made with crab, avocado, and cucumber. Most people in Japan have never heard of a California roll.

Warm-up   You may start the lesson in one of these ways:

- Have students look at the unit opener picture on page 107 and name as many of the foods as they can.
- Have a contest to see who can come up with the longest list of typically American foods. Set a time limit of three minutes. Find out who has the longest list, and write it on the board. Invite others to add items to the list. Discuss what part of the United States each food is found in. Help students make connections between foods and the ethnic groups that popularized them.
- Ask students to take turns describing their favorite American food and telling why they like it. Then help them make connections between the food and its origin (pizza, Italy; hamburgers, Germany; stirfry, China; tacos, Mexico; milkshakes, the United States).

Pre-Reading Activity   Ask students to scan the reading, looking for all the different ethnic groups mentioned. As students name the groups, make a master list on the board [the Germans, the Pueblo Indians (Native Americans), the Spanish, the English]. Next, ask them to scan the story again to find one food associated with each ethnic group. List the foods after the group names on the board and discuss them with the class.

Reading   Write these questions on the board and ask students to keep them in mind as they read:

What does history have to do with the foods people eat?
What are some foods that represent a mix of cultures?

Dictation   Use the last paragraph of the reading as a dictation exercise. Play the audio or read the paragraph aloud at normal speed, and have students take notes. Have them work together in groups to reconstruct the paragraph. Play the audio again before letting them check their answers in the book.

Journal   Write about your favorite food. Tell when and where you first tasted it, what else you like to eat with it, and whether you think it is a healthy food or not.

Chapter Nine Answer Key

Vocabulary
Meaning, p. 110
1. d   2. b   3. a   4. a   5. b   6. b   7. c   8. b   9. a   10. b

Word Building, p. 112
1. a. historical b. history   2. a. cooked b. cooking
3. a. influence b. influential

Comprehension
Looking for the Main Ideas, p. 112
1. d   2. c   3. a

Looking for Details, p. 113
1. T   2. F   3. F   4. F   5. T   6. F   7. T   8. T   9. T   10. F

Making Inferences and Drawing Conclusions, p. 113
Possible answers:
1. The foods in each area were influenced by the ethnic background of the people living there.
2. The history of an area describes the ethnic background of the people who settled the area and brought their food customs with them.
3. Spicy seasonings were common in Native American and Spanish dishes.
4. People like to eat these hearty foods when the weather is cool, as it usually is in New England.
5. One might find German food, since many Germans settled in the Midwest.

Writing
Model Essay, p. 115
Thesis statement: first sentence in paragraph 1
Paragraph 2 topic sentence: first sentence in paragraph
Paragraph 3 topic sentence: first sentence in paragraph
Paragraph 4 topic sentence: first sentence in paragraph

Exercise 1, p. 118
1. In New Mexico, fresh fruit is popular for dessert, whereas in New England, pies are often served.
2. In New Mexico, peppers and corn are popular as vegetables, while in New England, potatoes and carrots are eaten.
3. Whereas in New Mexico, chicken and beef appear in many recipes, in New England, fish is popular in many dishes.
4. The British put milk in their tea, while the Chinese drink it plain.
5. Whereas the Chinese love to stir-fry and deep-fry, the Vietnamese prefer to steam food or eat it raw.

6. The Chinese and Vietnamese use chopsticks that are about nine inches long and round at the eating end, while the Japanese prefer shorter chopsticks that have a pointed end.

Chapter Nine Assessment Answer Key

Vocabulary
1. d   2. b   3. b   4. a   5. c   6. d   7. a   8. d   9. c   10. b

Grammar/Language
1. c   2. d   3. b   4. b   5. b   6. d   7. b   8. a   9. a   10. a

Chapter Ten

Tea Anyone?

Audio CD, Track 10

Teaching Hints

Here are some interesting facts about tea:

- Aside from water, tea is the most widely consumed beverage in the world.
- A cup of tea contains from one half to one third as much caffeine as a cup of coffee.
- Medical researchers have determined that drinking several cups of green tea every day may decrease a person's chance of getting heart disease.

Warm-up   You may start the lesson in one of these ways:

- Hold a tea-smelling experiment in your class. Bring in several different types of tea in containers marked A, B, C, etc. Invite students to smell each of the teas and comment on them. At the end, tell them the name and origin of each one.
- Invite students to describe how tea is prepared and drunk in their home cultures. Add some interesting notes such as the following:

In the Middle East, some people drink tea through a sugar cube held between the teeth.
One Japanese tea (kukicha) is made from roasted twigs and branches from tea bushes, as well as the tea leaves.

Reading   To help students get a general idea of the information in the reading passage, ask them to read paragraphs 2 and 6. Then ask:

In what countries is tea-drinking especially popular? (Britain, China, Japan)
Which countries have especially interesting tea-drinking customs? (India, Burma, Thailand, Morocco)

Then write the following questions on the board, and ask students to read the whole passage:

What was tea first used for in China, and how was it served?
What are the steps in the Japanese tea ceremony?
How do the British prepare tea?

When students finish reading, discuss the questions with the class.

Journal   How important is tea in your life? Write about two or three times in the past when you remember having tea with someone. What was the occasion? What kind of tea did you drink? How did you feel?

 Video Activity   Make a list on the board of everything your students know about tortillas. Then make a list of questions about tortillas that they would like to know the answers to. Find out how many of the questions are answered in the video. Assign the remaining questions for homework. (See the video script on page 170.)

Internet Activity   Have students take careful notes on whichever tea ceremony they research. After they have discussed the research in groups, have students prepare a written summary with pictures for display in the classroom.

Chapter Ten Answer Key

Vocabulary
Meaning, p. 124
1. c   2. a   3. a   4. c   5. a   6. b   7. d   8. b   9. b   10. d

Word Building, p. 125
1. a. popularity b. popular   2. a. formality b. formal
3. a. polite b. politeness

Comprehension
Looking for the Main Ideas, p. 126
1. b   2. a   3. a

Looking for Details, p. 126
1. T   2. T   3. F   4. F   5. F   6. T   7. F   8. F   9. T   10. F

Making Inferences and Drawing Conclusions, p. 127
Possible answers:
1. Because tea was originally considered a medicine, it was served with much ceremony to show respect.
2. People have been drinking tea in Britain for many years, so it has become a tradition.
3. It gives people an opportunity to sit and talk.
4. It not only warms the body, but also provides a chance for the person drinking it to stop rushing around and calm down.
5. It may help them pause and become more thankful for the little things in life—like a good cup of tea.

Writing
Exercise 1, p. 130
1. Although many people drink coffee, the British are tea drinkers.
2. Although in Asia, people drink tea plain, the British prefer tea with milk added.
3. Even though most people make tea from tea leaves, the Burmese eat tea leaves as salad.
4. In Asia and Europe, tea is usually made in a ceramic or china teapot, although in Morocco, a brass or silver teapot is used.
5. Coffee has been regarded as the most popular beverage in the United States, even though soft drinks are consumed twice as much.

Do you know these food facts? p. 133
1. c   2. c
3. b (It is believed that Marco Polo brought this idea back from China.)
4. a   5. b   6. c   7. a

Video Activity, p. 34
1. Tortillas are round flat discs made from ground corn or wheat. They look like thin pancakes.
2. a. 50 billion   b. corn   c. the Spanish word *torta,* which means small cake
d. 1,500   e. lard or vegetable oil
3. Tortillas are inexpensive, nutritious, and low in fat (or fat free). They are easy to make and to store. They stay fresh for quite a long time and can be eaten with a wide variety of foods like vegetables or cheese or meat. They can be eaten hot or cold.

Chapter Ten Assessment Answer Key

Vocabulary
1. d   2. c   3. c   4. b   5. b   6. d   7. c   8. d   9. b   10. a

Grammar/Language
1. F   2. F   3. T   4. F   5. T   6. F   7. T   8. F   9. F   10. T

Chapter Eleven

Our Changing Language   Audio CD, Track 11

Teaching Hints

The readings and follow-up activities in this unit are about how changes in language affect people. Here are some interesting facts about how English has changed over the years:

- Many Native American words (for example, *Manhattan, squash, barbecue, canoe,* and *toboggan*) have been adopted into the English language.
- In the eighteenth century, immigrants from Scotland and Ireland settled in the Ozark Mountain region of the United States. Because of the relative isolation of the inhabitants, the dialect of English spoken there today still contains traces of eighteenth-century British pronunciation and word usage, which sound strange to other Americans.

Warm-up   You may start the lesson in one of these ways:

- Ask students to study the writing on page 135 and identify as many of the languages as they can (Hebrew, Arabic, Chinese, Greek, Armenian, Japanese). Invite them to share anything they know about these alphabets and languages.
- Write the following sentences on the board, and help students discover the nonsexist forms in parentheses:

  Everybody should hang his (his or her) coat in the closet. (All should hang their coats in the closet.)
  The repairman (repairperson) will fix the lock.
  Medical science has benefited men (people) everywhere.
  Call your doctor and leave him (him or her) a message.

Pre-Reading Activity   After doing the pre-reading activity in the book, read aloud some of the sentences from the reading passage that contain sexist terms and invite students to suggest nonsexist alternatives. List these pairs of sexist and nonsexist forms on the board and have students compare their ideas with those in the reading.

Reading   After they have completed the vocabulary and comprehension questions, ask students to read the passage on their own, underlining the main idea in each paragraph. When they finish, have students exchange their ideas with a partner and discuss them together.

Journal   Find examples of sexist language (in English or in your own language) in the newspaper or other media. How do you feel about these expressions? What should be done about them?

Culture Cue   Discuss the idea that learning to use egalitarian and nonsexist language is an important part of the task of an advanced English language learner. This skill is extremely important if students wish to function effectively in English-only situations, especially on the job.

Chapter Eleven Answer Key

Vocabulary
Meaning, p. 138
1. d   2. a   3. c   4. b   5. d   6. a   7. c   8. c

Word Building, p. 139
1. a. sensitivity b. sensitive   2. a. respect b. respectful
3. a. awareness b. aware

Comprehension
Looking for the Main Ideas, p. 140
1. d   2. a   3. c

Looking for Details, p. 140
1. The new names are sanitation worker and attendant.
2. An unmarried woman was called a spinster.
3. Today's job title for mailman is mail carrier; for watchman, it is guard.
4. We say Newsmaker of the Year.
5. Stewardesses are called flight attendants, laundresses are called laundry workers, and maids are called houseworkers.
6. The words *chair, fisher,* and *drafter* seem awkward.
7. We say *humankind* instead of *mankind.*

Making Inferences and Drawing Conclusions, p. 141
Possible answers:
1. Older people may fight these changes because they have a hard time getting used to them.
2. The new words are more accurate.
3. As we develop new attitudes toward people, the words used to describe them have to change.
4. Nonsexist job titles help to give both men and women a greater variety of employment opportunities.

Writing
Model Essay, p. 143
Thesis statement: last sentence in paragraph 1
Paragraph 1 topic sentence: first sentence in paragraph
Paragraph 2 topic sentence: first sentence in paragraph
Paragraph 3 topic sentence: first sentence in paragraph
Paragraph 4 topic sentence: last sentence in paragraph

Exercise 1, p. 146
1. Language changes as society changes. As society changes, language changes.
2. Words are added to the language every day as new things are invented. As new things are invented, words are added to the language every day.
3. There is a need to change some job titles as women are entering areas that were once thought of as men's jobs. As women are entering areas that were once thought of as men's jobs, there is a need to change some job titles.

Chapter Eleven Assessment Answer Key

Vocabulary
1. b   2. a   3. d   4. d   5. a   6. b   7. c   8. c   9. a   10. a

Grammar/Language
1. T   2. T   3. F   4. F   5. T   6. F   7. T   8. T   9. F   10. T

Chapter Twelve

English Around the World   Audio CD, Track 12

Teaching Hints

Here are some interesting facts about world languages:

- Over one billion people speak Mandarin Chinese, making it the most widely spoken language in the world. It is followed by English (over 500 million people), Hindi (almost 500 million people), and Spanish (over 400 million people).
- English is the official first language or one of several official languages in over 70 countries (including Fiji, Nigeria, and Singapore), but in some of these places very few citizens speak it.

Warm-up   You may start the lesson in one of these ways:

- Ask each student to bring to class a native language newspaper or magazine. Conduct a contest to see who can find the most borrowed English words in three minutes. As you check student responses, write the words on the board and discuss them with the class.
- Ask each student to brainstorm a list of English words that have become part of her or his native language over the years. On the board, make a column head for each language represented in your classroom and list the words. Discuss what types of words are most commonly borrowed from English (technical or scientific terms, references to popular culture, etc.).

Reading   Ask students to read the first sentence of each paragraph to get a general understanding of the reading passage. Then ask students to read the entire story on their own. When they finish, ask students to think of three questions about the reading.

Additional Discussion Questions   You might use one of these questions for a class discussion:

Why do you think English has spread so quickly in the last 50 years?
How do you think the Internet affects the spread of English?

Journal   For one week, every time you hear or see an English word that is commonly used in your native language, write it in your journal. At the end of the week, divide the words by category: sports, science, clothing, etc. Then write a paragraph describing the kinds of English words that are most commonly borrowed in your language.

Culture Cue As explained in the reading, some English words change their spelling and pronunciation when they are borrowed by another language. Be careful to avoid labeling such changes as incorrect. When words are borrowed by another language, they conform to the rules of that language.

Video Activity Find out how familiar students are with smiley faces. How many students use them? Are they useful? Why or why not? Then read the questions and check the vocabulary before watching the video. (See the video script on page 171.)

Internet Activity You might have students use the gender-specific problems and solutions as the basis for in-class role playing. Suggested keywords: *sexism, language.*

Chapter Twelve Answer Key

Vocabulary
Meaning, p. 151
1. b   2. d   3. a   4. a   5. b   6. a   7. d   8. a

Word Building, p. 152
1. a. understandable b. understood   2. a. spoken b. Speaking
3. a. threat b. threaten

Comprehension
Looking for the Main Ideas, p. 153
1. d   2. a   3. b

Looking for Details, p. 154
1. English is the official language in over 40 countries.
2. The Swedish language has borrowed the plural -*s* form.
3. *Sweater* has been changed to *sueter* in Spain and rush hour to *rushawa* in Japan.
4. The French started a commission to stop the use of English words in the French language.
5. Gaelic is the native Irish language.
6. Language experts say that many languages are disappearing.

Making Inferences and Drawing Conclusions, p. 155
Possible answers:
1. France feels that the purity of its language is threatened.
2. English is the main language spoken in Ireland.
3. Gaelic may disappear.
4. Yiddish and some Native American languages are disappearing.
5. English words can describe scientific processes very clearly and quickly. However, borrowing English words may cause some traditional words and phrases to disappear from other languages.

Writing
Exercise 1, p. 157
1. effect, cause   2. effect, cause   3. cause, effect   4. effect, cause, cause

Exercise 2, p. 158

1. Sometimes English words are changed to make them more like the native language; consequently, they are easier to say and remember.
2. In France, where English is not spoken, many words are borrowed; therefore, a French worker looks forward to *le weekend.*
3. English words are becoming popular in other languages; consequently, some people are afraid that the purity of their language is threatened.
4. People have strong feelings about the importance of their language; therefore, there will be no universal language in the near future.

Do you know these facts about language? p. 161

1. b   2. a. ketchup b. disco c. boss d. karate e. robot f. shampoo
3. b   4. c   5. c

Video Activity, p. 162

1. Answers will vary.
2. *a jest* (noun): a joke
   ironic (adjective): written or spoken in such a way that the audience knows
      that the writer/speaker means the opposite of what he or she says.
   a phenomenon (noun): an unusual thing or event
   a frown (noun): a sad or unhappy facial expression
3. a. ten b. frowning c. 700 d. they add expression
4. Answers will vary. Scott Baumann, who is credited with inventing them, believes good writers can express themselves without using smiley faces. David Sanderson thinks they are here to stay.

Chapter Twelve Assessment Answer Key

Vocabulary
1. a   2. a   3. b   4. d   5. c   6. b   7. d   8. a (or b)   9. c   10. b

Grammar/Language
1. T   2. F   3. T   4. T   5. T   6. F   7. T   8. F   9. F   10. T

Chapter Thirteen **Zoos** **Audio CD, Track 13**

Teaching Hints

The readings and follow-up activities in this unit explore some positive and negative effects of human alteration of the world's natural environment. Chapter Thirteen discusses the pros and cons of zoos. Chapter Fourteen presents the pros and cons of growing and consuming genetically modified food. Use the unit opener photo on page 163 to elicit from students a list of environmental concerns affecting the world today. How many of those concerns are represented in this seemingly idyllic picture? Here are some interesting facts about zoos:

- The largest zoos in the world are the Berlin Zoo in Germany (13,000 animals), the Bronx Zoo in New York (6,000 animals), the San Diego Zoo in California (4,000 animals), and the Pretoria Zoo in South Africa (3,500 animals).
- The oldest zoo in the world is the Vienna Zoo in Austria, which opened in 1752.
- The Singapore Zoo doesn't use fences. It separates the animals from the humans through the use of deep moats or ditches, some of which are filled with water.

Warm-up You may start the lesson in one of these ways:

- Bring in pictures of endangered species such as the black bear, the blue whale, the bison, the bottlenose dolphin, and the cheetah. Ask students what they think humans can do to prevent these species from dying out. Ask what role they think zoos play in preserving endangered species.
- Have students work in small groups to list the problems that are causing some animal species to die out. Ask them to think of at least three solutions for each problem.
- Have students imagine that they could choose 10 animals to be saved from extinction. Which animals would they choose and why?

Pre-Reading Activity Before students read, ask them to scan the reading, looking for the names of specific animals. Write the names on the board (polar bear, golden lion tamarin monkey). Next, ask them to look at these names again and find out what problem each animal has. (The polar bears get zoochosis and pace back and forth. The monkeys die when they are released back into the wild.)

Extension Activity After reviewing the answers to the comprehension questions, ask pairs of students to work together to make up one more question, which one of the students then asks the class. The other students should answer the question and say whether it was a general, detailed, or inference question.

Journal Write a paragraph about a visit to a zoo—either a recent visit or one that took place when you were a child. What were your reactions to seeing the animals in captivity? How were the animals being treated?

Chapter Thirteen Answer Key

Vocabulary
Meaning, p. 166
1. pacing up and down   2. instinct   3. an endangered species
4. extinct   5. dignity   6. was founded   7. conserve
8. database   9. confined   10. adapt

Word Building, p. 167
1. a. risk b. risky   2. a. entertainment b. entertaining
3. a. survive b. survival

Comprehension
Looking for the Main Ideas, p. 168
1. b   2. a   3. c

Looking for Details, p. 168
1. London   2. Zoological Society   3. *Animal Rights*
4. lack of space, lack of interest, an unsuitable diet
5. pacing up and down, rocking from side to side
6. they have been confined in a small area for 28 years
7. 10,000   8. pets, zoos   9. 30 survived   10. did not move

Making Inferences and Drawing Conclusions, p. 169
Possible answers:
1. They no longer behave the way they did in the wild.
2. The animals no longer look proud and happy.
3. Among other things, they can lose their ability to survive in the wild.
4. We can work to pass laws that halt the pollution and destruction of natural habitats.
5. People are becoming more aware of the importance of treating animals in a humane way.

Writing
Model Essay, p. 171
Paragraph 1 thesis statement: last sentence in paragraph
Paragraph 2 topic sentence: first sentence in paragraph
Paragraph 3 topic sentence: first sentence in paragraph
Paragraph 4 topic sentence: last sentence in paragraph

Exercise 1, p. 173
1. F   2. O   3. F   4. F   5. O   6. F   7. F   8. O

Exercise 2, p. 174
1. R   2. R   3. R   4. NR   5. NR   6. NR

Chapter 13 Assessment Answer Key

Vocabulary
1. c   2. a   3. c   4. b   5. b   6. d   7. a   8. d   9. c   10. b

Grammar/Language
1. T   2. F   3. F   4. T   5. F   6. F   7. T   8. T   9. T   10. T

Chapter Fourteen

Genetically Modified (GM) Food

Audio CD, Track 14

Teaching Hints

Here are some interesting facts about genetically modified (GM) food:

- GM seeds are made and patented by three large multinational companies and are often expensive to buy.
- Genes from GM crops can be transferred to conventional crops by the wind, tractors, or bees.
- Some examples of GM food are wheat that is resistant to pesticides, a tomato that ripens more slowly, a potato with more protein (the "protato"), and rice with extra vitamin A.

Warm-up   You may start the lesson in one of these ways:

- Have students look at the picture on page 177 and share what they know about organic food. (It is produced without the use of chemical fertilizers, hormones, or genetic engineering.) Ask them to list organic foods that are available in their community. Make a list of possible problems in determining whether food is really organic or not.
- Ask students to bring in ingredient labels from foods containing corn, soybeans, milk, or cottonseed oil (breakfast cereals, baked goods, frozen pizza, etc.). Ask students to locate these ingredients on the labels. Explain that some ingredients may have been produced using genetic engineering.

Reading   Have students read the selection all the way through without stopping, to get a general idea of what it is about. Play the audio or read the text aloud as they are reading. Before a second reading, ask:

Which paragraph gives us statistics about where GM crops are grown worldwide? (paragraph 5)
Which paragraph discusses the importance of GM crops to poorer countries? (paragraph 2)
In which paragraphs are specific genetic modifications of food discussed? (paragraphs 3 and 4)
Which paragraphs tell how genetic modifications work? (paragraphs 3 and 4)

Then have students reread the passage on their own.

Journal   For one week, whenever possible, check the labels of things you eat and drink at home or in restaurants, as well as anything you buy at the grocery store. Keep a list of items you think may be GM foods. At the end of the week, write about how you feel about eating these foods.

CNN.com   ### Video Activity   Discuss some of the ways in which food safety is checked in your country. How important are government regulations on how food is produced? Read the questions and explain any difficult vocabulary before having students watch the video. (See the video script on page 172.)

Internet Activity   Do a class survey to see who is in favor of GM foods and who is against them. Then ask some students to volunteer to research the opposite viewpoint in order to broaden their understanding of the issue.

Chapter Fourteen Answer Key

Predicting, p. 177
1. e   2. c   3. f   4. b   5. a   6. d

Vocabulary
Meaning, p. 180
1. pest   2. weed   3. nutritional value   4. exceed   5. scarce
6. absorb   7. developing countries   8. herbicides   9. resistant
10. crops

Word Building, p. 181
1. a. insects b. insecticides   2. a. nutritious b. nutritional
3. a. production b. produces

Comprehension
Looking for the Main Ideas, p. 181
1. a   2. a   3. d

Looking for Details, p. 182
1. The increase in world population will be mostly in developing countries.
2. Forty thousand people die from hunger each day.
3. The most common genetic modification is herbicide-resistant plants.
4. GM cotton is an example of a plant resistant to herbicides.
5. GM rice contains vitamin A.
6. GM potatoes might contain less starch.

Making Inferences and Drawing Conclusions, p. 182
Possible answers:
1. GM foods can resist diseases and insects and grow faster than regular plants.
2. Most of the development in these countries takes place in cities, so many people go there looking for work.
3. The population is growing quickly, and there is a limited amount of land and water.
4. Farmers can make more money with GM foods.
5. Long-term scientific studies must be completed before we will know about any possible risks of GM foods.

Writing
Exercise 1, p. 184
Statements 2 and 3 use reliable sources.

Do you know these interesting facts about animals? p. 187
1. b   2. b   3. c   4. d   5. a   6. c

Video Activity, p. 187

1. Possible answer: Aventis developed Starlink to resist damaging insects.
2. *a debacle* (noun): a disaster
   an allergen (noun): something that causes an allergy
   a moratorium (noun): a temporary stoppage
3. (1) e, (2) c, (3) a, (4) b, (5) d
4. Possible answers: Starlink provides an example of the possible risks of GM food. Whether the advantages of GM crops outweigh the disadvantages is open to argument. One reason environmentalists want a moratorium on them is to try to answer this question.

Chapter Fourteen Assessment Answer Key

Vocabulary
1. a   2. c   3. b   4. b   5. c   6. a   7. d   8. c   9. d   10. b

Grammar/Language
1. T   2. F   3. F   4. F   5. F   6. T   7. T   8. T   9. F   10. T

| **Chapter Fifteen** | **A Poem** | **Audio CD, Track 15** |

Teaching Hints

Unit Eight focuses on two literary genres—poetry and fables. Use the unit opening photo to ask students about books or poetry they have read in English. Ask students to bring in one book that they would recommend to the class, and then compile a reading list of recommended books. Here is some information about Carl Sandburg, the author of the poem in this chapter:

- Carl Sandburg (1878–1967) was born in Galesburg, Illinois, to poor Swedish immigrants.
- He was a central figure in the "Chicago Renaissance," a movement that expressed the new tone of American life in the twentieth century, and he played a significant role in the development of American poetry from 1910 to 1960.
- His poetry uses the ordinary language of the people to connect the traditions of America's frontier past to the industrial present.

Warm-up   You may start the lesson in one of these ways:

- Discuss the pictures on page 190. One is an example of ancient Egyptian hieroglyphics; the other is a Latin inscription. Both languages are no longer spoken.
- Brainstorm with students a list of ways poetry is different from prose. Accept all reasonable answers and list them on the board. The list may include

    The ends of lines rhyme.
    It's about feelings like love or hate.
    It's difficult to understand.

    Review the list and lead students to understand that their statements are true of some poems some of the time, but there are many different types of poems.

- Write the words *rhyme, rhythm, form,* and *imagery* on the board. Elicit definitions of each from students, adding your own explanations as necessary. (*Rhymes* are words that echo each other, like *bell* and *tell. Rhythm* is the beat or flow, including the amount of time between words as they are read aloud. *Form* is the length of the lines and how they are arranged on the page. *Imagery* is the pictures the words make in your mind.)

Return to your notes on the board after completing the exercises based on the Carl Sandburg poem.

Reading   Ask students to close their books as you read the poem aloud or play the audio. After the first reading, ask simple comprehension questions, such as

> What is the poem about? (languages, how languages change)
> What is language compared to? (a river flowing down a mountain to the ocean)

Then have students open their books. As you read the poem aloud again, ask them to follow along, looking for answers to the above questions and the following question:

> What verbs and other phrases describe what happens to languages over time? (breaking, changing, moving, crossing borders, mixing, die like rivers, wrapped around your tongue, broken to shape of thought, shall be faded hieroglyphics, is not here to-morrow)

After reading the poem and answering the vocabulary and comprehension questions, return to the predicting exercise on page 190 and explore some of these images more thoroughly. Have students write their own poems about language in groups or individually for homework, using their answers to the exercise.

Journal   Write about your favorite native-language or English-language poem. Explain why you like the poem. Include the name of the poem, the author's name, and a brief description of the rhyme (if any), rhythm, form, and imagery used.

Chapter Fifteen Answer Key

Vocabulary, p. 192
1. Whereby   2. course   3. border   4. handle   5. fade
6. Hieroglyphics   7. valley   8. wrap around

Comprehension
Analyzing Images, p. 193
1. b   2. a   3. b   4. d   5. a

Understanding the Poem, p. 194
Possible answers:
1. It flows easily from place to place, and its qualities change over time.
2. It flows along without set borders.
3. Languages die like rivers because each language flows into other languages as rivers flow into oceans.
4. Language is like the wind because it may exist at one moment but then die and be gone.

Recognizing Style, p. 195
Possible answers:
1. The words have a flowing rhythm. There are many images (word pictures) in the writing. For example, language is seen as a river flowing down a mountain.
2. Some lines are long, and some are short. Some lines end in punctuation, and some don't.
3. There are a few long lines mixed in with a lot of short lines.

Writing

Exercise 1, p. 196
Possible answers: 1. an old car   2. a plant without water   3. little jokes
4. a brick house   5. the sky

Exercise 2, p. 197
Possible answers: 1. a word game   2. learning to dance with words
3. the dances

Chapter Fifteen Assessment Answer Key

Vocabulary
1. b   2. a   3. d   4. d   5. b   6. c   7. c   8. b   9. a   10. d

Grammar/Language
1. T   2. F   3. T   4. F   5. T   6. F   7. T   8. F   9. T   10. T

Chapter Sixteen

A Fable   **Audio CD, Track 16**

Teaching Hints

Here are some interesting facts about fables:

- Aesop, an ancient Greek writer, wrote over 640 fables. His fables have been around for over 3,000 years, but every day people from schoolchildren to philosophers still contemplate the messages contained in his stories.
- One popular North American fable concerns a man named Paul Bunyan, who is said to have been a giant. According to the fable, he was so large that his footprints formed the Great Lakes and he was able to create the Mississippi River with his plow.

Warm-up   You may start the lesson in one of these ways:

- Point out that every culture in the world has its own fables. Asians have the Jataka stories; Native Americans in the Southwest have the Tricky Coyote stories. Ask students to describe some of the fables from their home cultures. Then elicit from students the definition of a fable (a story that demonstrates a moral truth).
- Divide the class into groups. Write a few proverbs on the board:

  More haste, less speed.
  Better safe than sorry.
  Too many cooks spoil the broth.
  Don't cry over spilled milk.

  Ask each group to write a short story illustrating the truth of one of the sayings. Have each group read its story to the class. The other groups have to guess which proverb each story illustrates.

Reading Explain that this fable, like most fables, is a very brief story told in chronological order. Point out that the story is intended to leave the reader with a clear and simple moral lesson. Ask students to look for the moral of the story as they read the fable.

Additional Discussion Questions

What is the effect of having the two people take refuge and meet in a cave? (It emphasizes the fact that they are both facing a similar problem.)
Why do you think the untouchable was so afraid to be touched? (Maybe he preferred to remain isolated because he was afraid of change.)

Journal Describe a time when you made a choice that later turned out to be a wrong decision. What did you learn from this experience? Summarize the moral of your story in one sentence.

CNN.com Video Activity Before showing the video, ask students what they think the typical poet is like. Have them describe his or her character and appearance. Then compare their ideas with the personality and appearance of the poet who appears in the video. Replay important segments of the tape so that students can answer the questions. (See the video script on page 173.)

 Internet Activity Students can use cue words such as "famous poets" or the name of an individual poet to find biographical information on the Internet. Some well-known poets are Eliot, Longfellow, Keats, Shelley, and Rosetti.

Chapter Sixteen Answer Key

Vocabulary, p. 200
1. honorable   2. precede   3. audacity   4. envy   5. an outcast
6. take refuge   7. stumble   8. precisely   9. totter   10. draw back
11. lay in another field

Comprehension
Understanding the Story, p. 201
1. The traveler goes into a cave.
2. An untouchable man is there already.
3. The man is warming himself by a fire.
4. The traveler sits on the other side of the fire.
5. The other man has the same feelings as the traveler.
6. There are no physical differences.
7. The traveler touches the untouchable.
8. Nothing happens after the traveler touches the untouchable.

Analyzing Ideas, p. 202
1. a   2. b   3. b   4. d

Recognizing Style, p. 203
Possible answers:
1. It takes place in India. Because there are untouchables and mountains in the story we know that the country is India. The clues are general. The writer chose them to make the story more universal.
2. None of these three things happened. The questions are exaggerated in tone. They emphasize the moral of the story.
3. The characters are surprised when nothing happens, but the writer is not. The writer conveys his opinion by simply telling the story and not commenting on the characters' thoughts or actions. This style is effective because it allows the truth to come through without making the reader feel that the writer is preaching to him or her.
4. The untouchable represents humility, and the traveler represents fairness.

Do you know these interesting facts about literature? p. 205
1. b   2. c   3. a   4. a   5. c   6. c

Video Activity, p. 205
1. Answers will vary. Many people fear or dislike poetry, perhaps because they find it hard to understand.
2. *toil* (verb): work
   obscurity (noun): darkness, lack of popularity
   awe (noun): wonder and dread or fear (adjective form: *awesome*)
3. a. $50,000 b. sunset and wind c. Clinton d. coffee houses e. facts
4. Possible answers: These natural phenomena are familiar. Poets can express complex emotions or ideas by comparing them to familiar things.

Chapter Sixteen Assessment Answer Key

Vocabulary
1. a   2. b   3. a   4. b   5. c   6. d   7. c   8. d   9. c   10. a

Grammar/Language
1. b   2. c   3. b   4. c   5. d   6. a   7. a   8. b   9. c   10. d

4 ■ HINTS/KEY

Chapter 1　Artists

Teaching Hints

The readings in this chapter encourage students to think about different types of art and talk about what art is. Reading 1 focuses on the life and works of one artist, Frida Kahlo. Reading 2 discusses digital photo illustration as an art form.

Two of the most important art movements of the past 150 years are Impressionism and Expressionism:

Impressionism (late 19th century): This movement started in France and focused on the artist's "impression" of reality. Light and color were important. Monet, Gauguin, and van Gogh were impressionists.
Expressionism (20th century): This movement started in Europe and focused on the artist's "expression" of emotion. The inner experience was important. Kahlo was an expressionist. Other expressionists include Gustav Klimt (Germany), Henri Matisse (France), and Wassily Kandinsky (Russia, Germany).

Reading 1　Frida Kahlo, p. 4　Audio CD 1, Track 2　

Warm-up　You may start the lesson by asking one of the following questions:

- What catches your eye in this self-portrait? What characteristic of the artist stands out? Do you think she is beautiful? Do you like the frame around the head? Why or why not?
- Imagine your self-portrait. What facial characteristic would be the most important? With what would you surround yourself?

Focus Questions　Write these questions on the board. Ask students to skim the reading passage. Have them discuss, in small groups, what they found.

What were some of the main influences on Frida's life?
Why do you think she became an artist?

Extension Activity　Have students, in pairs, write five to seven wh- questions (who, where, when, which, why, etc.) they would ask Frida if she were alive today. Then select one student to be Frida. The rest of the class should interview her, using the questions they created. If the class is large, divide it into groups of six to eight, with one student in each group selected to be Frida.

Additional Discussion Questions

What kind of art is popular in your country?
Do you enjoy going to art museums? Why or why not?

Journal   Write about your favorite artist. Why is he/she your favorite?

Reading 1 Answer Key: Frida Kahlo

Pre-Reading Activity, p. 2   **Audio CD 1, Track 1**

1. O'Keeffe   2. Monet   3. van Gogh   4. Dali   5. Gauguin

Vocabulary, p. 7
1. b   2. c   3. a   4. b   5. c   6. d   7. a   8. d   9. c   10. a

Vocabulary Extension
Part A, p. 8

Possible answers:

1. c	radical	**look**	*movement*	*ideas*
2. d	notorious	**group**	*reputation*	*criminal*
3. e	fatal	**accident**	*injury*	*wound*
4. a	celebrated	**artist**	*musician*	*painting*
5. f	emotional	**turbulence**	*life*	*pain*
6. b	elaborate	**decoration**	*design*	*painting*

Part B, p. 9
Possible answers:
1. In what way did Frida have a <u>radical</u> <u>look</u>?
2. Why did Frida join a <u>notorious</u> <u>group</u>?
3. How did Frida have an <u>accident</u> that was nearly <u>fatal</u>?
4. Which <u>celebrated</u> <u>artist</u> did she marry?
5. In what way was her life <u>emotionally</u> <u>turbulent</u>?
6. How did people know that Frida had <u>elaborate</u> <u>decoration</u> on her bed?

Comprehension
Main Ideas, p. 9
1. The main idea of paragraph 3 is how Frida Kahlo's life was influenced by her having polio at the age of six.
2. Paragraph 9 is mostly about the terrible bus accident in which Frida was badly injured.
3. Line 1 states the main idea of paragraph 11.
4. Sentences 1 and 2 contain the main idea in paragraph 12.

Details, p. 9
1. d   2. b   3. a   4. c   5. c   6. b   7. b   8. a   9. d   10. d

Inferences, p. 11
The statements that can be inferred are 1, 2, 3, 6, 7, and 9.

Warm-up   You may start the lesson by saying one of the following:

- Look at the picture. Do you think it is a painting? Why or why not?
- Give the picture a title. Explain why you gave it your title.

Focus Questions   Write these questions on the board. Ask students to skim the reading passage. Have them discuss, in small groups, what they found.

How have digital images changed traditional photography?
Is digital photo illustration an art form? Why or why not?
How have movies and television contributed to the development of digital photo illustration?

Extension Activity   Ask students to bring in a postcard, picture of a painting, photo, or digital illustration they like. Put the pieces on the wall, with a blank piece of paper under each one. Have the students move around the classroom and write, under each picture, one or two words to describe it. Then discuss the results. Why did the students choose those words?

Additional Discussion Questions

Can you imagine having a job in the field of digital photo illustration? Why or why not?
Do you think digital photo illustration will ever replace photography? Why or why not?

Journal   Which requires more creativity: painting or photography? Why do you think so?

 Video Activity   Ask students to list characteristics of modern art. Do they know the names of any modern artists? Show a short segment of the video that features one of Pollock's paintings (or bring in a postcard or picture). Ask students for their opinions, and compile a list of adjectives that could describe Pollock's art. Review the questions and vocabulary before watching the video. (See the video script on page 174.)

Internet Activity   Ask students to brainstorm a list of artists from their native countries. Have them search the Internet for information about one or two of the artists to share with the class.

Reading 2 Answer Key: Digital Photo Illustration

Vocabulary, p. 15
1. bridge the gap   2. b   3. periodical   4. a
5. a   6. a   7. c   8. genre   9. b   10. c

Vocabulary Extension
Part A, p. 17

Possible answers:

1. d	digital	**photography**	*camera*	*images*
2. f	technological	**development**	*advancements*	*industries*
3. a	preconceived	**boundaries**	*ideas*	*notions*
4. e	linear	**process**	*argument*	*thinking*
5. b	human	**perception**	*fallibility*	*productivity*
6. c	creative	**potential**	*processes*	*challenges*

Part B, p. 17
1. Photography changes as new <u>technological</u> <u>developments</u> are introduced.
2. The computer can open up a lot of <u>creative</u> <u>potential</u> for artists.
3. <u>Digital</u> <u>photography</u> has helped to change the way we view art.
4. Conventional photography is a <u>linear</u> <u>process</u>.
5. The mass media have a great influence on <u>human</u> <u>perception</u>.
6. We are no longer limited by <u>preconceived</u> <u>boundaries</u> between art and photography.

Comprehension
Main Ideas, p. 18
1. M   2. S   3. M   4. S   5. M   6. M   7. M   8. S

Details, p. 19
1. 1839   2. "From today painting is dead."   3. painting
4. periodicals   5. printing papers   6. stored   7. photographers
8. nineteenth century   9. drawing; painting   10. original

Inferences, p. 20
1. F   2. F   3. I   4. I   5. I   6. I   7. I   8. F

Writing
Writing a Summary, p. 21, Reading 1
Sample:

Frida Kahlo is Mexico's most famous female painter. She survived polio, a nearly fatal bus accident, and the emotional difficulties of her marriages to the artist Diego Rivera. She began painting when she was confined to bed after a bus accident. The physical and emotional pain in her life, as well as her strong spirit, contributed to her brilliant paintings. She was inspired to look inside and express her feelings in her art.

Paraphrasing, p. 21, paragraph 2, Reading 2
Sample:

According to Gardiner, advancements in technology determine changes in the field of photography. The first photographic prints, in the nineteenth century, led to pictures in books and magazines. Soon it was possible for the public to make their own photographs with simple cameras and fast printing papers. Business and industrial uses of photography affected not only photographic sizes and shapes but also new technological developments. The belief that art and technology are separate is fading as technology improves and becomes more user-friendly, less expensive, and, therefore, more available to the public.

Exercise 1, p. 25
Sentences 1, 3, 5, 8, and 12 are thesis statements.

Exercise 2, p. 26
1. a. The topic is a comparison between being an onlooker and being a true observer of art.
   b. The first sentence is the thesis statement.
   c. The writer begins with a strong opinion.
2. a. The topic is the definition of art.
   b. The last sentence is the thesis statement.
   c. The writer begins with a question.
3. a. The topic is the relationship between madness and creativity.
   b. The last sentence is the thesis statement.
   c. The writer begins with a quotation.

Exercise 3, p. 28
Possible answers:
1. III. Each child gets more individual attention.
2. III. People exercise less.
3. III. There are differences in transportation.
4. III. Information from all over the world can be easily accessed.
5. III. You can improve your physical health.

Exercise 4, p. 30
Samples:
1. To sum up, defining art is becoming more and more difficult. As technology is connecting the world, people are widening their understanding of art by learning more about art from other parts of the world. Secondly, art of this century cannot be conveniently characterized and classified. Finally, art is being created from previously unimagined sources, one of the most widespread being electronic images. In the future, the search for a definition of art will probably become even more complex.
2. In conclusion, the connection between the artist's emotional state, whether stable or unstable, and his or her creativity serves to increase the observer's awareness that what characterizes an artist's work often relates to his or her inner world. Many famous artists who have suffered great hardships have overcome their misfortunes and transformed their emotions into brilliant art that can touch the observer deeply.

Video Activity, p. 31
1. Jackson Pollack and Frida Kahlo were both rebellious, irreverent, controversial, original, and self-assured as painters.
2. *daunting:* intimidating, frightening
   colossal: very large
   unbridled: wild, uncontrolled
   irreverent: not respectful of authority
3. a. False (105)   b. True   c. False   d. False   e. True
4. Answers will vary.

Chapter One Assessment Answer Key

Reading 1 Vocabulary
1. b   2. c   3. a   4. a   5. a   6. d   7. b   8. d   9. d   10. c

Reading 2 Vocabulary
1. c   2. b   3. b   4. a   5. d   6. c   7. b   8. a   9. c   10. a

Language/Writing
1. c   2. a   3. d   4. d   5. c   6. c   7. a   8. b   9. c   10. d

Optional Question
1. The topic is Cubism.
2. The thesis statement is the last sentence: *These broken images popular in cubist art suggested a new kind of reality.*
3. A question is the device used to grab the reader's attention.

Teaching Hints

The readings in this chapter discuss historical aspects of English language development. Students will consider and discuss what they know about the background of their own language, as well as about English. Reading 1 deals with the history of English spelling. Reading 2 discusses the historical development of two words used in English.

- Do you know where the first printing press was invented? In China. The Chinese used wooden blocks to hand print in the 9th century and moveable type imprinted with thousands of Chinese characters around the year 1040, more than 400 years before Johannes Gutenberg's printing press. Gutenberg printed the Bible in 1454.
- Who is Geoffery Chaucer? Geoffrey Chaucer (ca 1343–1400) is considered one of the greatest poets in English literature. His major work, *The Canterbury Tales,* is a collection of twenty-four stories written in verse. Each story is told by one of a group of pilgrims making their way to Canterbury in Kent. The pilgrims include characters from all walks of life—for example, a knight (a soldier), a nun, a miller, a physician, a clerk. The stories give vivid and often humorous insights into the daily life and politics of the times. Chaucer wrote in English at a time when French was still the official language of the government. He helped to establish the rebirth of English as a national language and as a language of great literature. *The Canterbury Tales* was widely read, and it was the first nonreligious work to be printed in England by William Caxton (in 1478).

Reading 1

Spell It in English, p. 35   Audio CD 1, Track 5

Warm-up   Write the first word of each of the first five lines of the poem on p. 33 on the board in a column: Whilom, Ther, Of, And, That. Then play the first five lines of Audio CD 1, Track 4. Ask students to try to complete the lines while listening. Play the track several times. Then have students, in pairs, compare their answers and guess the meaning of the passage. Finally, listen to the modern version (the last four lines of the audio track). Compare the meaning to the interpretation on the board. What was difficult to guess?

Focus Questions   Write these questions on the board. Ask students to skim the reading passage. Have them discuss, in small groups, what they found.

Why is English spelling so confusing?
What is the connection between the invention of the printing press and English spelling?
What is "spelling reform"?

Extension Activity   Conduct a spelling bee, using the italicized words (*dough, bough, rough, colonel, ache,* etc.) from the reading. Divide the class into two groups. Ask one member of one team to spell a word. If the spelling is correct, 1 point is given to the group. If it is incorrect, the group is not given a point and a member of the other group is asked to spell the word. Continue asking one group and then the other to spell the words, and keep a running score.

Additional Discussion Questions

Do you use alternative spelling when you email or write text messages on your cellular phone? What are some examples? (Often people drop vowels to shorten words or use alternative spelling to shorten what they are saying, such as C U 2nite (for "see you tonight"). Do you think some of the alternative spellings may become acceptable ways to spell words in the future? Why or why not?

English has many homonyms (words that sound the same but are spelled differently)—for example, *to, too, two* and *bear, bare*. Think of some more homonyms with your partner. Write a list on the board. Are there also homonyms in your language?

Journal Choose one of the following topics:

- If a native English speaker were to learn your language, what do you think she or he would find most difficult about it? Why?
- Can you think of any words from other languages that are used in your native language? Do you know how they became common in your language?

Reading 1 Answer Key: Spell It in English

Pre-Reading Activity, p. 34
1. a. correct   b. bachelor   c. superintendent   d. excerpt   e. correct
f . tariff   g. occurrence   h. newsstand   i. correct   j. correct
2. color/colour, center/centre, behavior/behaviour, theater/ theatre, jail/gaol, judgment/judgement, program/programme, skillful/skilful, check/cheque, draft/draught

Vocabulary, p. 38
1. c   2. d   3. a   4. d   5. b   6. c   7. b   8. a   9. d   10. c

Vocabulary Extension
Part A, p. 40

			Possible answers:	
1. c	official	**language**	*title*	*regulation*
2. f	standard	**spelling**	*pronunciation*	*measurement*
3. b	punishable	**offense**	*crime*	*behavior*
4. e	phonetic	**system**	*spelling*	*symbol*
5. d	ongoing	**process**	*story*	*problems*
6. a	major	**change**	*discussion*	*developments*

Part B, p. 40
1. Spelling reform continues to be an <u>ongoing process</u>.
2. <u>Standardized spelling</u> was introduced with the first dictionaries.
3. It is unlikely that there will be any <u>major changes</u> in English spelling now.
4. Spelling did not represent the <u>phonetic system</u> of English.
5. Middle English became the <u>official language</u> of Britain by the 14th century.
6. Webster wanted to make the use of nonstandard spelling a <u>punishable offense</u>.

Comprehension
Main Ideas, p. 41
1. a   2. b   3. d

Details, p. 42
1. The Celtic language was a combination of the early forms of Irish, Scottish, and Welsh.
2. The Romans, the Germanic tribes, the Norsemen, and the French were all conquering peoples whose languages influenced the development of the English language.
3. English was mostly a spoken language before the invention of the printing press.
4. The typesetters of the 1500s weren't very helpful in making spelling standard because they were very careless with their spelling. They changed the spellings of words to make them fit on the lines. Sometimes they made up their own spellings, and different printers spelled words differently, depending on what they liked.
5. Samuel Johnson gave English its first great dictionary.
6. Noah Webster favored a more simplified, phonetic spelling system.
7. Shorthand, which was invented by Isaac Pitman, is a system in which symbols represent words, phrases, and letters.
8. Spelling reform associations simplified the spellings of many words.
9. The word *their* in the last sentence of paragraph 11 refers to *catalogue* and *dialogue.*
10. We are not likely to see major changes in the way words are spelled because people are most comfortable with what is familiar to them.

Inferences, p. 43
1. c   2. b   3. c   4. a

Reading 2
Coconut and Satellite, p. 45   Audio CD 1, Track 6

Warm-up   You may start the lesson in one of the following ways:

* Bring in pictures of recognizable objects from a magazine. Give each pair of students one magazine picture and ask them to identify the object. Then have them write a paragraph telling the story of where the word came from. Encourage them to be creative!
* Write a list of words on the board that you are sure no one can define. Put students in pairs and assign one word to each pair. Ask students to write down what they think the definition of the word is. Then share the real definitions. Was anyone close to the real meaning? Were there any definitions that sounded logical but were wrong?

Focus Questions   Write these questions on the board. Ask students to skim the reading passage. Have them discuss, in small groups, what they found.

What is the relationship between a coconut and a bogeymen?
What is the old name for *satellite?*
What was the function of a satellite?

Extension Activity   Choose one of the following:

* Share with students the fact that some countries currently have institutions whose job it is to make decisions about language, such as correct spelling,

whether or not to admit new words into the language (such as new technological terms or words from other languages), and even grammar rules. Some examples are the Real Academia Española in Spain and the Académie française in France. Then ask students: What are the pros and cons of institutions like these? Does your country have an institution like this? If so, what do you know about it?

• In advance, prepare a list of words and/or phrases that students are familiar with. Ask one student to come to the front of the class, and show him or her one of the words. The student must describe the word to the class while the rest of the class tries to guess it. For example, if the word is *language,* the student might say, "It's how we communicate. Examples are English, Spanish, Chinese. You can write it and speak it. . . ." Once someone guesses the word, it becomes another student's turn to come to the front. If the class is small, repeat the process until each student has a turn. If the class is large, repeat the process several times.

Additional Discussion Questions

What are some English words that are used in your language? Make a list on the board.

Why is it valuable to study old forms of English, such as the kind of English Chaucer used?

Journal   Select two or three of these terms: *discotheque, hot dog, automobile, philosopher, radio, radar, ok.* Look in a dictionary or on the Internet to find out where they came from and write about the information you find.

Video Activity   Play the video or part of the video without sound and ask students to answer these questions:

Where is this report taking place?
Are they talking about something that happened recently or in the past?
What do you think the video is about?

Review the questions and vocabulary before watching the video again. (See the video script on page 175.) Then play the video with sound and compare students' conclusions with what it is really about.

Internet Activity   Have students use the Internet to find out what a "spelling bee" is. What do you do at a spelling bee? What is the history of the spelling bee?

Reading 2 Answer Key: Coconut and Satellite

Vocabulary, p. 46
1. c   2. metropolis   3. b   4. unrest   5. b
6. a   7. a   8. c   9. revived   10. b

Vocabulary Extension
Part A, p. 48
1. resemble   2. adopt   3. threaten   4. surround
5. revive   6. revolve (about/around)

Part B, p. 48
1. Whom do you most <u>resemble</u>?
2. What expressions have you recently <u>adopted</u>?
3. What fashions have been <u>revived</u> recently?
4. How many planets that <u>revolve</u> around the sun can you name?
5. What <u>threatens</u> our planet the most?
6. What kinds of people usually <u>surround</u> movie stars, princes, and presidents?

Comprehension

Main Ideas, p. 49
1. M   2. S   3. M   4. S   5. S   6. S   7. M

Details, p. 50
1. coco; skull   2. two eyes and a mouth
3. coconut; the bogeyman, or coco   4. economic unrest; government
5. walk the streets of the capital without an escort   6. armed bodyguards
7. attendant   8. commerce; science   9. personal guards
10. Johannes Kepler; Jupiter

Inferences, p. 51
1. F   2. I   3. I   4. F   5. I   6. I   7. F   8. I   9. F   10. I

Writing

Writing a Summary, p. 53, Reading 1
Sample:

According to *Spell It in English,* there is a historical explanation for the inconsistency of English spelling. Before English became a written language, it was influenced by the languages of many European invaders and diversified by the various regional dialects within England. These factors created a language of many sounds, leading to different interpretations of how words should be spelled. Later, dictionaries helped standardize spelling, but there continued to be different ideas about correct spelling. Efforts to reform spelling continue to this day and will continue in the future as English, including its spelling, continues to evolve.

Paraphrasing, p. 53, paragraph 1, Reading 2
Sample:

According to Vanoni, Rome has had more world power than any other city in history. It was the center of Western culture for over one thousand years. Eventually, dissatisfaction with the economic situation as well as an unstable political situation caused the power of the Roman Empire to decrease.

Student Essay Follow-Up, p. 55
1. The writer is trying to explain the development of the written Chinese language.
2. The thesis statement is the last sentence of the introductory paragraph:
Chinese is one of the world's oldest languages, and its written form, like that of most languages, developed from the pictograph.
3. Yes, time signals are used through each phase of the process.
   Paragraph 2: 5,000 years ago
   Paragraph 3: Then, after a few centuries
   Paragraph 4: Later
4. The topic sentence in each body paragraph (paragraphs 2, 3, and 4) is the first sentence. The topic sentences are supported by the details in the body paragraphs.
5. The process of development is clear.

Exercise 1, p. 58

The first European to discover the Amazon River was Spanish explorer Vicente Pinzon <u>in</u> <u>1499</u>. He had been on Columbus's first voyage seven years earlier and was <u>still</u> determined to find a route to the Orient. <u>After</u> he sailed into the mouth of the Amazon and looked at the mighty river ahead of him, he thought he had gone around the world and hit the Ganges River in India. He stopped at some islands in the mouth of the river and <u>then</u> sailed on.

Forty-three years <u>later,</u> <u>in 1542</u>, Francisco de Orellana became the first European to travel the entire river, although that was not what he set out to do at all. <u>When</u> a Spanish expedition became stranded in the jungles of Eastern Peru, Orellana was sent down the Napo River to find food. But starvation, sickness, and Indian attacks took place, and Orellana couldn't get back upriver. Instead, he followed tributaries to the Amazon, and <u>during</u> 16 months of incredible hardships, he and what was left of his party made it all the way to the sea.

In <u>1561</u>, the notorious Lope de Aguirre traveled the Amazon <u>while</u> on the run from Spanish troops. He left a trail of death and destruction throughout the Amazon all the way to the sea.

No one traveled the entire river <u>for</u> another 76 years, <u>until</u> a Portuguese captain, Pedro Texeira, became the first to complete an upriver "ascent" <u>in 1637</u>.

Video Activity, p. 61

1. Answers will vary.
2. *tomb:* a place where someone is buried, usually with a monument above it
   to decipher: to decode, to figure out the meaning
   posthumous: after someone's death
   Coptic: Egyptian Christian
   pharaoh: an ancient Egyptian ruler
3. a. The symbols in ancient Egyptian writing represent meanings, not sounds. b. They have been found in tombs and in the pyramids.   c. A French code breaker deciphered the meaning of Egyptian hieroglyphics by using the Rosetta stone. (The Rosetta stone, now in the British Museum, was discovered by a French soldier in Egypt in 1799. The stone was carved with the same message in three different scripts: Egyptian hieroglyphs, a later form of ancient Egyptian, and Greek. The text was deciphered by Jean François Champillon, who studied the text for 14 years and published his results in 1822.)   d. They are in vertical or horizontal rows and can be read from right to left or from top to bottom. They are carved or painted on stone. Some are still brightly colored.
4. *Advantages of hieroglyphs:* The meaning is not lost, even though the sounds may be forgotten; the sound of the language can change, but the writing will remain the same; they might be used to communicate meaning between different languages; they look beautiful and are an art form.

   Disadvantages of hieroglyphs: You need many symbols; it takes a long time to write or carve the symbols; they take up a lot of space; it takes a long time to learn to read or write.

   Hieroglyphs were also used by the Mayan culture of Central America. These hieroglyphs have not yet been fully deciphered.

Chapter 2 Assessment Answer Key

Reading 1 Vocabulary
1. b   2. b   3. c   4. a   5. c   6. d   7. a   8. d   9. b   10. a

Reading 2 Vocabulary
1. a   2. c   3. c   4. b   5. a   6. c   7. d   8. c   9. d   10. b

Language/Writing
1. T   2. T   3. T   4. F   5. T   6. T   7. F   8. T   9. F   10. F

Optional Question
1. The writer's purpose is to describe the history of Gutenberg and his printing press.
2. The thesis statement is the last sentence of the introductory paragraph.
3. The time signals that are used through each phase of the process are as follows:
    body paragraph 1: later, around 1400, when, then, from 1438 to 1450
    body paragraph 2: then, first, in 1454
    body paragraph 3: final, in 1468
4. The topic sentences for each of the body paragraphs are as follows:
    body paragraph 1: sentence 1
    body paragraph 2: sentence 2
    body paragraph 3: sentence 1
    The topic sentences are all supported by the other sentences in the paragraphs.
5. The process of development is clear because the essay is in chronological order.

Teaching Hints

The readings in this chapter give information on how and why living things clean themselves or are cleaned. Reading 1 offers some interpretations and examples of personal cleanliness throughout history. Reading 2 focuses on examples of fish species that clean other fish and the process of cleaning.

- Did you know that, at the end of the Roman Empire, bathhouses were ordered to be shut down all over Europe because they were considered corrupt? However, the most northern countries—Finland, Estonia, and northern Russia—were so far away that they escaped this ruling. The operation of bathhouses in those countries has continued uninterrupted until today.
- Did you know that, in Finland, there are almost as many saunas (sweat baths) as cars? In 1998, there were 2.0 million cars and 1.6 million saunas. A sauna is a room that is heated to very high temperatures by a wood or coal stove. People take saunas for relaxing and cleansing. After sitting in the heat, people often jump into cold water or take a cold shower to cool off.

Reading 1   **Cleanliness, p. 64**   **Audio CD 1, Track 7**

Warm-up   You may start the lesson by asking one of the following questions:

- What are the differences between how the person in this photo is going to take a bath and how people in your culture take baths today?
- Would you like to take a bath in this way? Why or why not?

Focus Questions   Write these questions on the board. Ask students to skim the reading passage. Have them discuss, in small groups, what they found.

How have people in different cultures kept clean throughout history?
What significance has cleanliness had for people in different cultures throughout history?

 Extension Activity   Play the audio track, pausing at the end of each paragraph. Have students write a content question for the paragraph they just heard. Continue paragraph by paragraph until the end. Have students ask their questions to the class, and discuss the answers.

Additional Discussion Questions

What are the main functions of water? Generate a list with a partner. Then arrange the items in order of importance. Are there any other resources on earth that are more important, in your opinion? Why or why not?
What types of bathing products do you use when you take a bath or shower?

Journal   What are some ways to keep our environment clean? What do you do to keep your environment clean?

Pre-Reading Activity, p. 63
1. False   2. True   3. True   4. False   5. True   6. False

Vocabulary, p. 67
1. b   2. a   3. d   4. c   5. a   6. d   7. d   8. a   9. b   10. c

Vocabulary Extension
Part A, p. 68

Possible answers:

1. e	mental	**relaxation**	*ability*	*exercise*
2. a	medicinal	**treatment**	*herb*	*root*
3. f	archaeological	**evidence**	*survey*	*site*
4. b	social	**offense**	*blunder*	*activity*
5. c	religious	**overtones**	*service*	*art*
6. d	personal	**hygiene**	*belief*	*trainer*

Part B, p. 69
1. Ruins of many ancient civilizations show <u>archaeological</u> <u>evidence</u> of baths.
2. Bathing is a form of <u>mental</u> <u>relaxation</u>.
3. If you are sick, bathing can be a form of <u>medicinal</u> <u>treatment</u>.
4. In some cultures, bathing is not only for cleanliness, it also has <u>religious</u> <u>overtones</u>.
5. If your body smells, it can cause <u>social</u> <u>offense</u>.
6. <u>Personal</u> <u>hygiene</u> is more important in some cultures than in others.

Part C, p. 69
Answers will vary.

Comprehension
Main Ideas, p. 69
1. d   2. c   3. b

Details, p. 70
1. Over the centuries, the bathing habits of people have been influenced by religion, culture, and technology.
2. The Greeks' bathing habits differed from the Egyptians' in that the Greeks did not use soap. Instead, they put oil and ashes on their bodies, scrubbed with blocks of rock or sand, and scraped themselves clean with a curved metal instrument.
3. In the last sentence of paragraph 3, the word *them* refers to the Greeks.
4. First, Roman bathers entered a warm room to sweat and converse. Fine oils and sand were used to cleanse the body. Next, they went into a hot room for more sweating and talk, splashing with water, and more oils and scraping. Finally, the bathers concluded the process by plunging into a cool and refreshing pool.
5. The leaders of the Christian church discouraged bathing during the Middle Ages because they associated it with the corruption of Roman society and its baths.
6. Commoners found it difficult to bathe because there was no running water, the rivers were polluted, and soap was too expensive for them to afford, since it was taxed as a luxury item.
7. Europeans and Americans changed their cleanliness habits when it became known that filth led to disease and the governments of Europe and America began to improve sanitation standards. They built wash houses, and bathing began to be considered a good thing.

8. The Muslim tradition of using *hammams,* or sweat baths, for cleansing and as retreats and places for socializing was brought to Europe by the Crusaders and consequently influenced the use of thermal baths as therapy for a variety of ills.

9. The word *people* in paragraph 10, sentence 3, refers to Middle Easterners.

10. Two hygienic habits of the Japanese are removing their shoes and putting on special slippers before entering any house or building and washing extensively before meals.

Inferences, p. 71
1. c   2. b   3. d   4. b

Reading 2   Cleaner Fish, p. 73   Audio CD 1, Track 8

Warm-up   The picture on p. 73 shows a fish that cleans other fish. Ask students to describe the picture. Write *symbiosis* on the board. Give students examples of animals and/or plants that have symbiotic relationships, such as the clown fish and sea anemone, bees and flowers, the oxpecker (a parasite-eating bird) and zebra, intestinal bacteria and humans. Ask them to write a definition of symbiosis based on these examples.

Focus Questions   Write these questions on the board. Ask students to skim the reading passage. Have them discuss, in small groups, what they found.

Why must all creatures stay clean?
How does one fish clean another? Describe the process.
What are some of the characteristics of fish that are being cleaned?

Extension Activity   Listen to the audio track, stopping after each paragraph. Have the students write down a new vocabulary word or phrase they remember from each paragraph. Ask one student to state his/her word or phrase to the class and another student to give the meaning. Do this a few times before going on to the next paragraph and repeating the procedure.

Journal   Write about one or two things you learned from this reading that surprise or impress you.

CNN.com.   **Video Activity**   Have students work in pairs. Tell student A to face the video, and student B to turn his or her chair away. While watching the video, student A describes the pedal-powered washing machine to student B, and student B draws a picture of it. Then have all the students watch the video together and compare their drawings to the machine shown on the screen. Review the questions and vocabulary before watching the video again. (See the video script on page 175.)

 Internet Activity   Look up one of the cleaner fish mentioned in this reading (*Labroides dimidiatus,* goby, Senorita Fish, or another of the wrasse family). Find some details about their behavior that have not been mentioned in the reading. Share them with the class.

Culture Cue   Cleanliness is personal and has many different interpretations. Be aware of this when interacting with members of different cultures so as not to cause misunderstanding or offense. When discussing this topic, try to avoid stereotypes and labeling of behavior as clean or unclean.

Vocabulary, p. 76
1. d (or b)   2. b   3. groomed   4. a   5. a
6. b   7. c   8. a   9. c   10. the bulk of

Vocabulary Extension
Part A, p. 77

			Possible answers:	
1. d	modify	**behavior**	colors	habits
2. c	display	**ferocity**	friendship	hostility
3. f	perform	**a service**	a duty	a function
4. a	set up	**a station**	a company	a process
5. e	observe	**effects**	behavior	actions
6. b	prey on	**smaller fish**	animals	victims

Part B, p. 77
Possible answers:
1. Why do some of the aggressive fish have to <u>modify</u> their <u>behavior</u> in order to be cleaned?
2. When do the fish being cleaned <u>display</u> <u>ferocity</u>?
3. Why do the cleaner fish <u>perform</u> <u>a service</u> for some of the larger, aggressive fish?
4. Why do the cleaner fish <u>set up</u> <u>a station</u> where other fish can be cleaned?
5. Who <u>observed</u> <u>effects</u> of removing all the cleaner fish from one locality?
6. What are the names of some fish that <u>prey on</u> <u>smaller fish</u>?

Comprehension
Main Ideas, p. 78
1. S   2. M   3. S   4. S   5. M   6. M   7. S   8. M   9. S   10. S

Details, p. 79
1. shark; barracuda; moray eels
2. establish a cleaning symbiosis
3. pale brown; pink
4. suddenly closing its mouth, leaving only a small gap to allow the goby to escape
5. visit cleaning stations
6. six; Senorita
7. develop the fuzzy marks that are an indication of fungal infection
8. fungi; restore the fish to health
9. swimming in a vertical position, head downward, and undulating its body from side to side
10. small; cigar-shaped

Inferences, p. 80
1. I   2. F   3. I   4. I   5. F   6. F   7. F   8. I   9. F   10. I

Writing
Writing a Summary, p. 81, Reading 1
Sample:

The reading about cleanliness states that religion, culture, and technology have always exercised strong influences on hygiene. Baths existed in ancient times; the later Roman baths were extensive and ultimately corrupt. In reaction to this corruption, bathing was uncommon in the Middle Ages, but regained favor in the 1800s when it became known that filth led to disease. Personal hygiene is highly valued in Japan, and cleanliness is a religious requirement in the Middle East. There are clearly many different methods of and reasons for personal cleanliness.

Paraphrasing, p. 81, paragraph 2, Reading 2
Sample:
      According to Perry, most cleaners are fish. There are more than 45 known cleaner species. In order for cleaners to function, client fish must often change their normal behavior. Even aggressive fish let their cleaners safely clean them. The client fish help their cleaners by becoming still or slow-moving and allowing the cleaners safe access to all body parts. Some species have probably died out because they were unable to create a client-cleaner relationship. Without the benefit of cleaner fish, so many fish may have been harmed by fungal infection that the population could not survive.

Student Essay Follow-Up, p. 83
1. The thesis statement is the last sentence of the introductory paragraph: *In my country, Japan, our basic sense of cleanliness may be more clearly defined by looking at basic aspects of our lives such as our buildings, our food, and hygiene.*
2. To define cleanliness, the writer focuses on three aspects of life in Japan: buildings, food, and hygiene.
3. Yes, buildings, food, and hygiene are all developed in the body paragraphs.
4. All the ideas in paragraph 2 support and illustrate the topic sentence. Topic sentence: *Traditionally, it is the custom in Japan to keep our homes clean, since a clean house is a reflection of one's self.* Supports: *taking off our shoes; clean socks with no holes; changing into different slippers; bathrooms separated from the toilets; floors are clean.*
5. Answers will vary.

Exercise 1, p. 84
  1. Art is a means by which an artist graphically represents the world as seen through his or her own vision.
  2. Accurate
  3. Wind is one of the most powerful forces in nature and can be beneficial—for example, as a source of energy—as well as destructive, such as in storms.
  4. Powered flight, by adding an engine to a flying machine, is the means by which humans can fly, thus realizing man's fondest dream for thousands of years.
  5. A keynote address is a speech at the beginning of a conference or convention outlining the issues that will be considered.
  6. Accurate
  7. Mountain sickness is an impaired physical state marked by shortness of breath, nausea, and headache and caused by insufficient oxygen at high altitudes.
  8. Accurate
  9. Good sense is the ability to think and reason soundly, something everyone should hope to have.
10. Education is obtaining knowledge through instruction, which is the key to prosperity.

Exercise 2, p. 8

1. Space	*Literal Meaning:*	an open expanse; blank or empty area
	Extended Meaning:	Answers will vary.
2. Time	*Literal Meaning:*	a continuum in which events occur from the past through the present to the future
	Extended Meaning:	Answers will vary.
3. Smell	*Literal Meaning:*	the sense by which odors are perceived
	Extended Meaning:	Answers will vary.
4. Aggressiveness	*Literal Meaning:*	assertiveness; boldness
	Extended Meaning:	Answers will vary.
5. Modesty	*Literal Meaning:*	the condition of being humble, proper, and/or reserved
	Extended Meaning:	Answers will vary.
6. Respect	*Literal Meaning:*	esteem; regard
	Extended Meaning:	Answers will vary.

Exercise 3, p. 87
Possible answers:
1. *fanaticism:* excessive or irrational behavior
2. *loyalty:* faithfulness
3. *education:* the action or process of being given knowledge, instruction, or training, usually in school
4. *happiness:* joyfulness
5. *creativity:* originality; imaginativeness
6. *friendship:* a close, trusting, and warm relationship with another person
7. *independence:* freedom from the control of others
8. *leadership:* the ability to provide guidance to others

Video Activity, p. 90
1. Answers will vary.
2. *device:* machine or invention
   portable: easy to move
   durable: strong, long-lasting
   to refine: to improve, make perfect
3. a. People on an island with no electricity or plumbing might invent a machine like this.
   b. Two electrical engineering students at the Royal Melbourne Institute of Technology in Australia
   c. They used cheap, strong, lightweight materials. It costs $30.
   d. It does not use electricity, which is usually produced with products that pollute the environment, like coal or oil.
   e. Answers will vary.
4. Answers will vary

Chapter 3 Assessment Answer Key

Reading 1 Vocabulary
1. b   2. c   3. d   4. a   5. a   6. d   7. b   8. b   9. c   10. c

Reading 2 Vocabulary
1. c   2. b   3. b   4. a   5. d   6. a   7. d   8. a   9. d   10. c

Language/Writing
1. F   2. F   3. F   4. T   5. F   6. T   7. T   8. T   9. T   10. F

Teaching Hints

The readings in this chapter describe two groups, one that makes positive contributions to the world and another that was criminal. Reading 1 describes a worldwide emergency health care organization called Doctors Without Borders. Reading 2 describes a 17th- and 18th-century group of murderers in India, called Thugs.

- Did you know that the Amish *(aw-mish)* people, a group that came to the United States in 1927 from Switzerland, have worn the same kind of clothing for 270 years? The women wear dresses with long skirts and aprons and cover their hair with a scarf or hat, and the men wear hats, coats without collars and pockets, and pants that are held up with suspenders.
- Did you know that the Mormon religion was founded in 1830 in New York State and is now centered in the state of Utah? Mormons don't smoke or drink alcohol or caffeine. Ten percent of their income goes to their church—a practice called *tithing*. One result of tithing is that they extend financial support to church members who need help and do not make use of the country's federal assistance programs.

Reading 1

Doctors Without Borders, p. 94

Audio CD 1, Track 10

Warm-up   You may start the lesson in one of the following ways:

- Have students describe the pictures on p. 91. Where and who are these people? What do they appear to be doing? Ask them to write their own caption for each of the photos and share it with the class.
- Have students listen to or read the five descriptions of groups in the Activity on p. 92 (Audio CD 1, Track 9) and match the names with the descriptions. What are some characteristics that are true of all of these groups?
- Bring in—or have the students bring in—some pictures of people wearing traditional unique clothing, such as the Amish or Inuits. Put the pictures on the wall and have the students move around the classroom to view them. Discuss the students' reactions: What kind of a group might they be? Where might they be from? Why do they think so?

Focus Questions   Write these questions on the board. Ask students to skim the reading passage. Have them discuss, in small groups, what they found.

What is the philosophy of Doctors Without Borders?
How did the organization develop and how does it survive?
What is their procedure in a crisis?
What do they do besides providing medical care?

Extension Activity   Have students, in pairs, write five questions that they would ask a volunteer in the Doctors Without Borders organization. Then divide the class into groups of four or five, and select one student in each group to be the volunteer. The others in the group should ask the questions they have created.

Additional Discussion Questions

Many organizations, such as Doctors Without Borders, are formed with the goal of helping others. What benefits do such organizations have for the people who join them? What organizations have you heard of that you might like to participate in? Why?
Describe an organization that you would like to create. What would its purpose be?

Journal   Are there any aspects of Doctors Without Borders that impress you? Do you think that this organization is making a difference in the world? Why or why not?

Reading 1 Answer Key: Doctors Without Borders

Pre-Reading Activity, p. 92   **Audio CD 1, Track 9**
1. Scouts   2. Amish   3. Greenpeace
4. Salvation Army   5. Masons

Vocabulary, p. 96
1. b   2. a   3. c   4. d   5. b   6. a   7. a   8. b   9. a   10. d

Vocabulary Extension
Part A, p. 98

1. b	give emergency aid to	*victims of war*
2. f	take a	*professional approach*
3. a	deal with	*emergencies*
4. e	provide	*medical assistance*
5. d	maintain	*its independence*
6. c	live up to	*its ideals*

Part B, p. 98
Possible answers:
1. Why does Doctors Without Borders <u>give emergency aid to</u> <u>victims of war</u>?
2. Why did Doctors Without Borders want to <u>take a professional approach</u>?
3. How does Doctors Without Borders <u>deal with</u> <u>emergencies</u>?
4. To whom does Doctors Without Borders <u>provide</u> <u>medical assistance</u>?
5. Why is Doctors Without Borders allowed to <u>maintain</u> <u>its independence</u>?
6. How does Doctors Without Borders to <u>live up to</u> <u>its ideals</u>?

Comprehension
Main Ideas, p. 98
1. M   2. S   3. M   4. S   5. M   6. S   7. S   8. M   9. S   10. S

Details, p. 99
1. race; religion; political affiliation   2. France   3. New York
4. United Nations   5. nonprofit   6. 2,500   7. ideals   8. emergency kits

Inferences, p. 100
1. I   2. F   3. I   4. F   5. I   6. F   7. I   8. F

Stranglers in a Strange Land, p. 102

Warm-up   You may start the lesson in one of the following ways:

- Have students look at the picture and describe it. What are these people doing? What kinds of people do you think they are?
- Have students look at the title. What is the "Strange Land"? Do you know what "Stranglers" means? Do you think it is negative or positive? Why?
- Ask students: How would you defend yourself if you were attacked? Have you ever learned specific techniques for self-defense? If anyone in the class knows a type of martial art or other self-defense technique, you may ask them to demonstrate or describe it for the class.

Focus Questions   Write these questions on the board. Ask students to skim the reading passage. Have them discuss, in small groups, what they found.

What did the Thugs do?
How did they do this?
Why were they allowed to continue their actions for more than 100 years?
How were their activities finally stopped?

Extension Activity   Choose one of the following:

- Have students bring in the name and one or two characteristics of a well-known criminal organization in their country or in the world. Have them discuss their information in groups.
- Ask students: Why do some young people join criminal groups? What can be done to discourage them from doing so?

Additional Discussion Questions

Why do you think people join groups?
What are some ways you can help prevent crime in your neighborhood?

Journal   What are some different ways to learn about and practice self-defense?

Video Activity   Review the questions and vocabulary before showing the video. After students complete the task, show the video again and ask each student to make a list of the animals seen and mentioned in the video and then compare his or her list with a classmate's. (See the video script on page 176.)

Internet Activity   Provide the names of several local charities or volunteer organizations. Divide the class into groups; have each group research one organization and then share their information with the class.

Culture Cue   Be sensitive to different cultural practices concerning animals. For example, while it is illegal to hunt whales, many cultures still regard whale meat as a delicacy and eating it is a national custom.

Vocabulary, p. 104
1. a   2. d   3. b   4. c   5. a   6. d   7. c   8. b   9. a   10. c

Vocabulary Extension
Part A, p. 106
1. perform   *carry out*
2. go in advance   *send ahead*
3. eliminate   *get rid of*
4. help   *give a hand*
5. divide   *break up*

Part B, p. 106
Possible answers:
1. Why did the Thugs <u>carry out</u> these murders?
2. Why did they <u>send ahead</u> members of their group?
3. Why did they <u>get rid of</u> the first group?
4. How many people <u>gave a hand</u> in the murders?
5. Who finally <u>broke up</u> the organization?

Comprehension
Main Ideas, p. 106
1. The main idea of paragraph 5 is how the Thugs worked together to accomplish their criminal acts.
2. Line 1 states the main idea of paragraph 6.
3. Sentence 3 contains the main idea of paragraph 8.

Details, p. 107
1. The Thugs murdered travelers on Indian roads.
2. The Thugs murdered people supposedly to carry out the wishes of the goddess Kali.
3. The Thugs numbered in the tens of thousands.
4. The Indian authorities did nothing about the Thugs. They looked the other way, and some even offered protection for a price.
5. If travelers suspected a group of Thugs, another group would infiltrate them.
6. Thugs traveled with their victims to gain their friendship and confidence.
7. The murders usually occurred when the party rested at an appropriate spot.
8. Their weapon was a strip of twisted yellow or white silk knotted at one end with a silver coin consecrated to Kali.
9. In paragraph 8, the word *system* refers to the protection of the Thugs by corrupt rajahs, Indian chiefs, police, and local authorities.
10. Their confessions were stupefying because many Thugs proudly admitted to an unthinkable number of murders.

Inferences, p. 107
1. c   2. a   3. b

Writing

Writing a Summary, p. 109, Reading 1
Sample:

According the article, Doctors Without Borders is an organization of doctors and other medical professionals who offer emergency aid worldwide to victims of war, epidemics, and disasters. It began as a small volunteer organization over 30 years ago and is now funded by public donations that allow volunteers to receive stipends and provide money for better technology. Because Doctors Without Borders is an independent organization, members can and do speak out about human rights issues. The organization has had such an impact throughout the world that it won the Nobel Peace Prize in 1999.

Paraphrasing, p. 109, paragraph 5, Reading 2
Sample:

According to Milhomme, the Thugs worked together to accomplish their criminal acts and also relied on surprising their victims. Some members prepared murder and burial sites in advance, and others followed members who had found victims. If the Thugs who were accompanying the victims needed more aid in carrying out the murders, they left marks on the road that indicated to those behind them that they should catch up. Groups of Thugs replaced each other if the travelers became suspicious, and if travelers remained suspicious, Thugs watched them carefully from a distance while they planned their murder.

Student Essay Follow-Up, p. 111
1. The thesis statement is the last sentence of the introductory paragraph: *Most Vegans can be characterized by their avoidance of consuming animal foods and their derivatives, their avoidance of using products derived from animals, and their support for animal rights groups.*
2. The writer focuses on Vegans' avoidance of consuming animal foods and their derivatives, their avoidance of using products derived from animals, and their support for animal rights groups.
3. Yes, each of these characteristics is developed in the body paragraphs.
4. All the ideas in paragraph 2 support the main idea. Descriptive words such as *cruel* and *suffer* strengthen the dominant impression.
5. Dominant aspect or impression of the body paragraphs:
   Body paragraph 1: Vegans do not eat meat, fish, poultry, eggs or animals' milk and its derivatives such as yogurt, cheese, and butter.
   Body paragraph 2: Vegans avoid using any products derived from animals.
   Body paragraph 3: Most Vegans support animal rights groups.

Exercise 1, p. 113
Possible answers:
1. The Thugs were as cold-blooded as crocodiles.
2. The Thugs preyed on their victims like starving wolves.
3. The Thugs were as cunning as foxes.
4. Captain William Sleeman was as courageous as a lion.
5. The goddess Kali was as evil as the devil.
6. The organization spread as quickly as a wild fire.
7. The medical team is as efficient as a team of mountain lions.
8. Their work is as desperately needed as water in the desert.

Exercise 2, p. 114

1. This compares good (sheep) and evil (the Thugs/wolves). The Thugs look good, but underneath they are evil. The Thugs acted as if they were one with the travelers in order to kill them.
2. This compares the efficiency of the Thugs' communication system with radar, which is very precise. It shows that their communication was efficient, quick, and direct.
3. This compares the growth of Doctors Without Borders with the growth of a plant. As a plant's roots spread and grow, so did the organization.
4. The way the Thugs found and murdered their victims is being compared to the way tigers sit unseen and wait for the right moment to kill their prey.
5. This compares testimony (a statement of what was experienced) to a torch (a light that makes it easier to see). Giving testimony to make the experience public makes people aware of others suffering similar circumstances in other places.
6. This compares a knock on the door (signifying the appearance of help) to not losing hope.

Video Activity, p. 116

1. Answers will vary.
2. *flora:* plants (Latin)
   fauna: animals (Latin)
   poachers: people who hunt wild animals illegally
3. a. Bengal tiger   b. Black   c. ivory   d. mahogany   e. Thailand
4. Answers will vary.

Chapter Four Assessment Answer Key

Reading 1 Vocabulary
1. a   2. c   3. a   4. b   5. c   6. a   7. a   8. d   9. a   10. d

Reading 2 Vocabulary
1. d   2. b   3. c   4. c   5. a   6. c   7. a   8. b   9. a   10. d

Language/Writing
1. T   2. F   3. F   4. T   5. T   6. F   7. T   8. T   9. T   10. T

4 ■ HINTS/KEY

Teaching Hints

The readings in this chapter discuss theories of personality. Reading 1 focuses on different theories about the relationship between physical characteristics and personality. Reading 2 describes a theory claiming that differences in personality are based on psychological and physiological differences.

- After blood typing was discovered in the 19th century, theories began to emerge about the effect of different blood types on personalities. For example, people with type O blood tend to be independent and expressive and are risk takers. Those with blood type A are said to be careful, introspective, and structure-oriented, and blood type B personalities are characterized as emotional, sociable, and unconventional. It's said that people with type AB blood are rational, efficient, and personable.
- The Meyers Briggs type indicator test is a personality questionnaire that asks you to identify your reactions to certain situations in order to identify what type of person you are. The classifications are based on these categories: introversion, extroversion, intuitiveness, sensing, thinking, feeling, perceiving, judging.

Reading 1   **Body Language, p. 118**   **Audio CD 1, Track 12**

Warm-up   Find a simple personality quiz on the Internet or in a book. Bring it in for students to complete individually. Ask students if they agree with the outcome.

Focus Questions   Write these questions on the board. Ask students to skim the reading passage. Have them discuss, in small groups, what they found.

   What was William Sheldon's proposal?
   What are "body splits?"
   How does stereotyping relate to the topic?

Extension Activity   Choose one of the following:

- Play the audio track. As students listen to paragraphs 4, 6, 7, and 8, ask them to draw the shapes that describe the contents of the paragraphs. Then have them compare their drawings with classmates'.
- Have students, in groups of three to five, create their own personality tests. First, they select a category, such as colors, shapes, months of the year, or weather. Then they choose some items from that category and give them meanings that make sense to them. For example, common but very different Western associations with the color green are jealousy and relaxation. They can make up a simple story about the items so they represent personality traits. Have them give their test to another group.

Additional Discussion Question How, in your opinion, might stereotypes about the connection between body shape and personality be hurtful to the individual?

Journal   Explain which of the following you think is correct, and why:

- The body type determines the personality.
- The personality determines the body type.
- Body type and personality are unrelated.

Reading 1 Answer Key: Body Language

Pre-Reading Activity, p. 117
Answers will vary.

Vocabulary, p. 120
1. b   2. c   3. a   4. c   5. b   6. c   7. a   8. d   9. b   10. a

Vocabulary Extension
Part A, p. 122
1. active and <u>confident</u>   2. burdens and <u>troubles</u>   3. anger and <u>stress</u>
4. dominant and <u>forceful</u>   5. shy and <u>timid</u>   6. happy and <u>warmhearted</u>

Part B, p. 122
1. A person who is <u>confident</u> likes to talk a lot.
2. A <u>timid</u> person is afraid of everything.
3. A <u>warmhearted</u> person is very generous.
4. A person who uses strength to get his or her own way is <u>forceful</u>.
5. Someone with a stooped back usually has a lot of <u>troubles</u>.
6. If you are under a lot of <u>stress</u>, you will get sick more often.

Part C, p. 123
Answers will vary.

Comprehension
Main Ideas, p. 123
1. c   2. d   3. b

Details, p. 123
1. The relationship between physical characteristics and personality has been used to predict and explain the actions of others.
2. According to the Greek theory, there are four body fluids, each with its own related personality type: blood, producing a sanguine, or hopeful, temperament; black bile, producing a melancholic, or sad, temperament; yellow bile, producing a choleric, or hot-tempered, temperament; and phlegm, producing a phlegmatic, or lazy or slow, temperament.
3. William Sheldon divided people into three shapes: the endomorph, with an oval shape; the mesomorph, with a triangular shape and a muscular, firm, upright body; and the ectomorph, with a thin, fragile body.
4. The word *their* in paragraph 5, sentence 1, refers to researchers.
5. In the theory of "body splits," the upper body is expressive and relates our feelings to others through gestures and facial expressions.
6. The words *this theory* in paragraph 6, line 1, refer to the theory of "body splits."

7. According to the theory of "body splits," four clues to personality are weight distribution, muscular development, grace and coordination, and general health.
8. The front of the body is associated with our conscious self, the one we think about and show to others.
9. An energetic person may not be a good listener because it's hard for energetic people to sit still and they can sometimes be impatient.
10. The stereotype of fat people is that they are happy and warmhearted.

Inferences, p. 124
1. c   2. a   3. d   4. b

Reading 2   Extraversion and Introversion, p. 126

Audio CD 2, Track 1

Warm-up   You may start the lesson in one of the following ways:

• Make two cluster diagrams on the board, one with the word *outgoing* in the middle and the other with the word *shy* in the middle. Be sure that everyone understands the meanings of these words. Then write the word *party* over these clusters, and ask the students to come to the board and write adjectives or descriptive phrases for outgoing and shy people at a party. Discuss the results.
• Look at the chart on p. 126. Using the contents of the chart, move around the room and ask each student to describe himself or herself with two of the adjectives. When the process has been completed, find out whether the students in your classroom tend to share the same personality types. You may want to speculate on why this might be true.

Focus Questions   Write these questions on the board. Ask students to skim the reading passage. Have them discuss, in small groups, what they found.

What is a supertrait?
According to Eysenck, how do extraverts and introverts differ physiologically?
What part of Eysenck's theory is accepted today?

Extension Activity   You may start the lesson in one of the following ways:

• Play the audio track. Pause the tape or CD after each paragraph and have students, in pairs, write a phrase or sentence that expresses the main idea of the paragraph. Continue this procedure until the end. Then have students share some of their answers. Write some answers on the board. Indicate that this is the groundwork for a summary of the reading.
• Have students prepare a short skit or dialogue between an introvert and an extravert in a particular situation. Divide the class into pairs and assign a different situation to each pair (for example, at a party, at work, in the library). Then have students share their skit or dialogue with the class. It can be creative and humorous.

Additional Discussion Questions

Compare your school life to your life at home. Are you more extraverted or introverted in one place than the other? If not, why not? If so, why do you think this is true?

What professions do you think attract extraverts? Which ones attract introverts? Why?

Journal   Do you classify yourself as an extravert or an introvert? Why? Describe some of your characteristics.

CNN.com.   **Video Activity**   *Cultural background:* The Smithsonian, located in Washington D.C., is a group of national museums and research centers dedicated to art and design, history and culture, and science and technology. People of all ages visit the museums to see unique exhibits and learn new things about everything from art to early world cultures to scientific discoveries and advances. For example, the Museum of Natural History has a well-known dinosaur exhibit, and the Air and Space Museum houses the first airplane flown by the Wright brothers.

Review the vocabulary before watching the video. (See the video script on page 177.)

Internet Activity   Find out more about the connection between blood type and personality or between the hand and personality ("palmistry"). Share your information with the class.

Culture Cue   Be sensitive to different cultures' ideal body types when discussing the first reading. In addition, be aware that the Zodiac can be offensive to some religions. It is best to avoid discussing this as a way to assess personality.

Reading 2 Answer Key: Extraversion and Introversion

Vocabulary, p. 129
1. c   2. d   3. c   4. b   5. d   6. a   7. a   8. b   9. c   10. a

Vocabulary Extension
Part A, p. 130
1. watch	*observe*
2. have or own	*possess*
3. claim	*maintain*
4. suggest	*propose*
5. look for	*seek out*
6. choose	*select*

Part B, p. 131
1. An extravert <u>possesses</u> different personality traits than an introvert does.
2. Extraverts tend to <u>seek out</u> noisy situations.
3. Introverts usually <u>select</u> solitude.
4. Eysenck <u>observed</u> typical behavior of different personality types.
5. Eysenck <u>maintained</u> that people have different levels of cerebral cortex arousal.
6. Eysenck <u>proposed</u> a theory to explain the connection between cerebral cortex arousal and personality.

Part C, p. 131
Possible answers:
1. What kinds of personality traits do you <u>possess</u>?
2. What kinds of situations do you tend to <u>seek out</u>?
3. When do you select <u>solitude</u>?
4. How can we <u>observe</u> someone's personality?
5. What did Eysenck <u>maintain</u>?
6. What theory did Eysenck <u>propose</u>?

Part D, p. 131
1. *in*offensive person   2. *in*flexible boss   3. *im*practical way
4. *in*discreet manner   5. *in*fallible judge of character   6. *in*efficient worker
7. *ir*reproachable character   8. *ir*rational thinker   9. *im*patient onlooker
10. *un*enlightened colleague   11. *in*sincere woman   12. *in*consistent behavior
13. *in*corruptible officer   14. *in*decisive child   15. *in*elegant posture
16. *in*judicious judgment   17. *ir*responsible person   18. *im*personal judge
19. *un*bending father   20. *un*pretentious millionaire

Comprehension
Main Ideas, p. 132
1. The main idea of paragraph 1 is that Eysenck divided the elements of personality into various units based upon behavior.
2. Lines 1–3 state the main idea in paragraph 2.
3. Paragraph 3 is mostly about the characteristics of extraverts and introverts.
4. In paragraph 4, sentence 1 contains the main idea.

Details, p. 132
1. c   2. c   3. a   4. d   5. d   6. b   7. b   8. a   9. c   10. d

Inferences, p. 134
The statements that can be inferred are 3, 4, 6, 8, 9, and 10.

Writing
Writing a Summary, p. 136, Reading 1
Sample:

The reading *Body Language* states that people have always explored the relationship between personality and physical characteristics. One theory from the late 1940s, formulated by William Sheldon, associates certain temperaments with the basic body shapes of endomorphs, mesomorphs, and ectomorphs. Another theory states that the shape and condition of different body parts reflect certain personality traits. Although many theories make connections between temperament and body shape, some argue that these associations are stereotypical and have no real basis. Whether this is a real or perceived relationship, the topic continues to fascinate people.

Paraphrasing, p. 136, paragraph 4, Reading 2
Sample:

According to Burger, Eysenck regards the differences between extraverts and introverts as both behavioral and physiological. Initially, Eysenck believed that extraverts and introverts had different levels of cerebral cortex arousal—activity levels in the language, memory, and thinking part of the brain—when at rest. He reasoned that since extraverts are gregarious, they must have a lower cerebral cortex arousal, and therefore they constantly seek more stimulation. Introverts, on the other hand, would have a higher cerebral cortex arousal and thus make efforts to reduce their arousal level. This would explain why, in a noisy party environment, extraverts are comfortable and introverts uncomfortable.

Student Essay Follow-Up, p. 138
1. The thesis statement is the last sentence of the introductory paragraph: *These twelve astrological signs can be classified into the four elements in this world, which are wind, earth, fire, and water.*
2. The writer classified astrological signs into the four elements in the world: wind, earth, fire, and water.
3.

Category	Signs	Characteristics
wind	Gemini Libra Aquarius	natural-born debaters; more advantages than others in their careers; overcome difficulties easily; don't like steady jobs; like exciting jobs and challenges
earth	Taurus Virgo Capricorn	decisive, solid, immovable, patient; like routine and stable tasks; obstinate, loyal, reliable partners
fire	Aries Leo Sagittarius	impatient, in a hurry; strong desire for success; are often leaders; risk-takers, explorers, inventors
water	Cancer Scorpio Pisces	sensitive, artistic, creative, expressive; can be very close friends or relatives; romantic

4. The writer uses supporting examples for each element. See answer 3, above.
5. All members of my class fall under one of the elements because astrological signs, which relate to birth dates, cover all calendar dates.

Exercise 1, p. 139
1. *Motorcycle.* All the others have four wheels.
2. *Swimming.* All the others use a ball.
3. *Newspaper article.* All the others are forms of literature.
4. *By bus.* All the others are general forms of travel.
5. *Brilliance.* All the others are types of degrees teachers might have.
6. *Beachwear.* All the others are general styles of clothes.
7. *Tennis.* All the others do not require a ball.
8. *Monkey.* All the others are reptiles.
9. *Sugar.* All the others are major food types.
10. *Hallucinogens.* All the others are legal drugs.

Exercise 2, p. 140
1. level of intelligence of students   2. types of graders teachers are
3. shapes of people's faces   4. color of people's hair   5. types of drivers
6. types of food bats eat   7. types of burns   8. people's residential status

Exercise 3, p. 142
    According to Dr. Li Tao in his book *How to Read Faces,* people can be divided into two broad categories: those who are mentally inclined and those who are firmly practical. Mind-oriented people have balanced faces that can be divided into three roughly equal sections. <u>On the other hand</u>, physical types tend to have larger jaws and shorter faces. <u>In addition to</u> these two broad categories, Dr. Tao divides faces into five basic shapes. The <u>first</u> is the round face with strong bone structure. It is <u>typical of</u> a mentally active person with self-confidence, resistance to illness, and a potentially long life. <u>Next</u> is the diamond-shaped face, which indicates a generally warm, strong-willed, and lucky person. <u>Third</u> is the rectangular face, and <u>fourth</u> is the square face. <u>Whereas</u> the rectangular face indicates

creativity, intelligence, and self-control, the square face belongs to an honest, well-balanced person with leadership qualities. <u>Last</u> is the triangular face, with its wide forehead, prominent cheekbones, and pointed chin. <u>Besides</u> having a brilliant and sensual temperament, the triangular-faced person is intelligent and ambitious. <u>A good example</u> of such a person is the famous Elizabeth of Austria.

Video Activity, p. 145

1. Answers will vary.
2. *illusion:* false or deceptive image
   diversity: variety
   light-hearted: cheerful
   voyeurism: curiosity, desire to watch others secretly
3. a.   Answers will vary.   b. Some exhibits include a test that asks you to look at colors instead of words, a rotating tent that makes you think you are moving, and one that asks you to walk only on black squares.   c. Children say they learn and have fun at the same time. Adults say it is fun to participate in the exhibits and act like kids again.
4. Answers will vary.

Chapter 5 Assessment Answer Key

Reading 1 Vocabulary
1. d   2. a   3. b   4. c   5. c   6. d   7. d   8. a   9. c   10. b

Reading 2 Vocabulary
1. a   2. a   3. d   4. c   5. b   6. a   7. a   8. d   9. b   10. c

Language/Writing
1. c   2. b   3. d   4. a   5. a   6. a   7. d   8. b   9. c   10. d

Optional Question
2. Principle of classification: periods of time; *alternatively* does not fit
3. Principle of classification: types of fabric; *wood* does not fit
4. Principle of classification: personality traits/characteristics; *narrow* does not fit
5. Principle of classification: vegetables; *apples* does not fit

Teaching Hints

The readings in this chapter provide information about how shoes, trousers, and skirts have changed throughout history. Reading 1 traces the development of shoes—in particular, the various styles of the toe of the shoe. Reading 2 focuses on the evolution of trousers and skirts as worn by both men and women.

Do you know that American and British English use different words for many pieces of clothing? Here are some examples:

American English	British English
vest	waistcoat
pants	trousers
scarf	muffler
suspenders	braces
running shoes	trainers

Work environments often require that you dress differently than you would at home. What is the difference between a uniform, a dress code, and a dress-down day at work?

- A uniform is clothing that is the same for everyone. For example, bank workers and store assistants wear uniforms in Japan. Postal workers and restaurant servers wear uniforms in the United States. Many school children around the world wear uniforms.
- A dress code is a set of rules by which to dress. A workplace may have a dress code that says you must wear pants of a certain color or are not allowed to wear shorts.
- A dress-down day is a designated day (usually Friday) on which employees in many companies can wear casual clothes instead of more formal clothes. For example, during the week employees may follow a dress code that requires men to wear a suit and women a skirt and blouse, but on Fridays everyone is allowed to wear jeans, tennis shoes, and casual shirts.

Reading 1   The Toe of the Shoe, p. 148   Audio CD 2, Track 2

Warm-up   You may start the lesson in one of the following ways:

- Have students look at the pictures on p. 146 and answer these questions: Do you think these are shoes from the present or past? Who do you think might wear or have worn shoes like this? Here's where the shoes really came from (from top to bottom):
  China, 19th century; woman's shoe with central heel and fish-head toe
  Country unknown, 16th century; woman's bridged shoe
  India, late 19th century
- Create and conduct a survey about what the students look for when they buy shoes—for example, comfort, style, cheap price, or color. Make a list on the board. Then survey the class to find out which is the most important characteristic.

Focus Questions

Explain the practice of Chinese foot binding. Why was it popular?
What are some milestones in the history of pointed shoes?
What are some features of the women's shoe trend since the 17th century?

Extension Activity Choose one of the following:

- Have students look around their environment at the shoes people are wearing and answer the following questions: Are the shoes similar, or are there many types? Are the fashionable ones also the most comfortable, in your opinion? Do people of different ages tend to wear different kinds of shoes? Why do you think this is/is not true?
- Divide students into three to six groups and assign each group one type of shoe described in the reading. Ask students to find the paragraph in the reading that discusses the specific type of shoe and to draw a picture of it. Share the drawings with the class. Ask the students if these drawings represent how they imagine the shoe to look. Have they ever seen a shoe that looks similar? (The types of shoes described include women's shoes in ancient China, men's shoes in ancient Egypt, men's shoes in Europe during the 13th and 14th centuries, women's shoes in Europe during the 1500s, women's shoes in France during the 17th century, women's shoes in America during the 1930s.)

Additional Discussion Questions

Which shoes discussed in the reading do you think are the strangest? Why?
What do you like to wear on your feet? Why? Do you like to go barefoot? When and where do you go barefoot?
What do you think about women wearing high heels?

Journal Describe what's important to you when you go shopping for shoes or clothes.

Reading 1 Answer Key: The Toe of the Shoes

Pre-Reading Activity, p. 147
Answers will vary.

Vocabulary, p. 151
1. d   2. a   3. d   4. c   5. c   6. a   7. b   8. b   9. d   10. b

Vocabulary Extension
Part A, p. 153
1. notice   *ignore*
2. obey   *defy*
3. allowed   *forbidden*
4. intelligent *foolish*
5. awkward   *elegant*
6. survive   *die out*

Part B, p. 153
1. What kinds of fashions nowadays are <u>elegant</u>?
2. Why do some fashions quickly <u>die out</u>?
3. What fashions do you tend to <u>ignore</u>?
4. What kind of clothing is <u>forbidden</u> at your school or at work?
5. What kinds of school regulations do students often <u>defy</u>?
6. Do you mind looking fashionable but <u>foolish</u>?

Part C, p. 154
1. A gray-haired man   2. Rubber-soled shoes   3. Open-toed shoes
4. A long-sleeved shirt   5. A leather-strapped shoe   6. An open-necked shirt
7. A wide-shouldered man   8. A rosy-cheeked girl   9. Metal-framed glasses

Comprehension
Main Ideas, p. 155
1. The main idea of paragraph 2 is that a painful and crippling fashion for upper-class girls in ancient China was to bind their feet to make them small.
2. The main idea of paragraph 7 is stated in line 1.
3. Sentences 1 and 2 contain the main idea in paragraph 13.
4. Paragraph 15 is mostly about why humans follow fashions in footwear even when they are painful or dangerous.

Details, p. 155
1. c   2. a   3. b   4. c   5. b   6. d   7. b   8. a   9. c   10. d

Inferences, p. 157
The statements that can be inferred are 1, 2, 4, 6, and 9.

Reading 2   Trousers and Skirts, p. 158   Audio CD 2, Track 3

Warm-up   You may start the lesson in one of the following ways:

- Bring in—or have the students bring in—some magazine pictures of people or clothing from different places and times. Put the pictures on the wall and number each picture. Have students number a sheet of paper and move around the classroom, writing down the country or part of the world and the time they think the picture shows. Discuss the results. Why did the students make those choices?
- Ask students: Do people in the city dress differently than people in the country? If so, describe what each wears.

Focus Questions

What are the two basic types and the one intermediate type of clothing, and how are they characterized?
How did the Europeans and the Chinese regard robes and trousers, and why?
How did the wearing of trousers by women evolve in the West?

Extension Activity   Choose one of the following:

- Ask students about their ideas of dressing comfortably. Here are some questions to ask: What do you wear? Can you dress like this at all times in your culture? Do certain cultures put more value on fashion than others? Which cultures, in your opinion? Do certain cultures put more value on comfort? Which ones? Can you think of any reasons why this might be true?

- Write this well-known English expression on the board: *Clothes make the man.* Discuss with students what they think this means. Then divide the class into two sections and debate the topic. Each side should think of two or three reasons to support their position.

Additional Discussion Questions

What is considered formal and casual in your country?
Do people dress differently for certain occasions, such as a holiday, marriage, or funeral? When? What do they wear?

Journal   Describe your taste in clothes. How does it reflect your personality?

Video Activity   Review the questions and vocabulary before showing the video. Show the video again and have students write down which items (a) they would never wear, (b) they might wear, and (c) they would love to wear. Discuss why they made those choices. (See the video script on page 178.)

Internet Activity   Below are some idioms that relate to clothing. Have students find out what they mean by using the idiom as the keyword for a search or by first searching for an idioms web site by using the keyword "idiom."

If the shoe fits, wear it.	to be a shoe-in
to wear the pants in the family	to skirt an issue

Culture Cue   In many Muslim countries, it is not acceptable for women to wear clothing that does not cover up the body. It is important for women who visit these countries to be sensitive to this and dress appropriately.

Reading 2 Answer Key: Trousers and Skirts

Vocabulary, p. 161
1. a   2. indigenous   3. c   4. b   5. c   6. a
7. prudish   8. d   9. conspicuous   10. b

Vocabulary Extension
Part A, p. 162

			Possible answers:	
1. e	social	**status**	*occasion*	*event*
2. a	tailored	**clothes**	*suit*	*jacket*
3. f	nomadic	**way of life**	*people*	*culture*
4. b	masculine	**connotations**	*clothing*	*appearance*
5. d	conspicuous	**consumption**	*appearance*	*behavior*
6. c	unacceptable	**street wear**	*language*	*attitude*

Part B, p. 163
1. In Europe, wearing trousers had strong <u>masculine</u> <u>connotations</u>.
2. In China, robes and trousers indicated <u>social</u> <u>status</u>.
3. People in the north wore close-fitting <u>tailored</u> <u>clothes</u>.
4. Horseback riding was part of the <u>nomadic</u> <u>way of life</u>.
5. <u>Conspicuous</u> <u>consumption</u> in the 1920s included buying luxury fashion items.
6. Trousers were <u>unacceptable</u> <u>street wear</u> for women until the 1960s.

Comprehension

Main Ideas, p. 163

1. M   2. S   3. S   4. S   5. M   6. M   7. S   8. M   9. S   10. S

Details, p. 164

1. draped or wrapped; toga; sarong; sari   2. binary
3. cultural contact; population movement; invasion   4. social status
5. Persia; late prehistoric   6. barbarians   7. short; long
8. soldiers; masculinity   9. trousers; short skirts; class; gender
10. teenagers; college coeds; suburban housewives

Inferences, p. 165

1. I   2. F   3. F   4. F   5. I   6. I   7. F   8. I   9. F   10. I

Writing

Writing a Summary, p. 167, Reading 1
Sample:

   According to the article, shoes were created to protect the feet. However, they are also the best example of the silly or uncomfortable clothing humans tolerate in order to be fashionable. For hundreds of years, the Chinese bound girls' feet so that they could wear tiny shoes when they became women. From ancient times until only a few centuries ago, men wore shoes with various styles of extremely oversized toes, because these shoes were popular or a sign of status. In the 17th century, women started wearing the small, tight-toed shoes still popular today. Despite the discomfort and ridiculousness of many shoe styles throughout history, human beings continue to be slaves to fashion.

Paraphrasing, p. 167, paragraph 5, Reading 2
Sample:

   Based on Kidwell and Steele's research, they believe that pants had a definite masculine association in Europe, but this was not true in China. The masculine ideal in China—the scholar or government worker—wore robes. People in China who wore trousers included soldiers and both male and female peasants, so robes were associated with rulers and thus were accorded more status than trousers. Upper-class women wore trousers to ride horses and also for casual events.

Student Essay Follow-Up, p. 169

1. The thesis statement is the last sentence of the introductory paragraph: *In this essay, the rise and fall of short skirts and other features of fashion of the Twenties and Sixties will be compared and contrasted in relation to social changes and economic and political conditions.*
2. The fashions of the Twenties and Sixties will be compared and contrasted from the point of view of social changes and economic and political conditions.
3. In paragraph 2, the conditions mentioned that were similar for women in the Twenties and Sixties were female emancipation, electro-technological advances, and the continuing development of mass media.
4. The similarity discussed in paragraph 3 is the unisex type of beauty in the Twenties and Sixties. Women had short hair and short skirts.
5. Economic and political conditions influenced the end of short skirts in the Twenties and Seventies.
6. The topic sentence in paragraph 3 that shows comparison (similarity) is the first sentence: *In both the Twenties and the Sixties, a new accepted type of beauty was the unisex type; that is, girls strove to look as much like boys as possible.* The topic sentence in paragraph 4 that shows comparison (similarity) is the first sentence: *The fall of short skirts was influenced by economic and political conditions.*

Exercise 1, p. 170
Answers will vary.

Exercise 2, p. 174
1. Although foot-binding was a painful process for girls in China, they considered it a great honor.
2. Whereas women in China experienced inconvenience over shoes, in other parts of the world, men experienced inconvenience over shoes.
3. The long-toed shoe became foolish and ridiculous; likewise, the wide-toed shoe became just as foolish. (Note: The clause introduced by *likewise* shortens, or paraphrases, the first clause so as not to repeat it.)
4. Just as a law was passed to limit shoe-toe length, a law was passed to limit shoe-toe width.
5. Women wore moderately wide shoes; however, men went to extremes with the fashion.
6. In Europe, robes were associated with femininity; in contrast, robes were associated with social status in China.
7. In China, rulers wore robes, whereas peasants and soldiers wore trousers.
8. At the end of the 18th century, high-born and middle-class women wore long skirts, while peasant and working-class women wore shorter skirts.
9. The fashion of short skirts ended in the 1920s because of troubled economic and political conditions, just as short skirts went out of fashion in the 1970s for the same reasons.

Video Activity, p. 177
1. Answers will vary.
2. *well-heeled:* wealthy, well off
   bridle: here, a leather strap on a shoe, but usually headgear on a horse attached to straps called reins
   to rip off: to steal
   exotic: unusual, usually foreign
3. a. feet   b. People have different perceptions about what is beautiful.
c. the night sky   d. 20   e. fish skin (from a sting ray) and amethysts

Chapter 6 Assessment Answer Key

Reading 1 Vocabulary
1. b   2. c   3. b   4. a   5. c   6. a   7. a   8. d   9. a   10. a

Reading 2 Vocabulary
1. c   2. d   3. a   4. d   5. b   6. a   7. d   8. a   9. c   10. c

Language/Writing
1. F   2. T   3. T   4. F   5. F   6. F   7. F   8. T   9. T   10. F

Teaching Hints

The readings in this chapter are concerned with nutrition—in particular, the unhealthy effects of substances that humans introduce into food and into animals involved in food production. Reading 1 informs the reader about chemicals that are added to food and focuses on three unsafe food additives. Reading 2 discusses health concerns related to BST, a hormone given to cattle to increase milk production.

Did you know that sugar, honey, and salt are natural preservatives? High levels of sugar can be used in jams, boiled sweets, and chocolates to preserve them. Honey is a natural food preservative that also prevents bacteria and infection. Salt has been used since ancient times to preserve meat. It is even believed that salt contributed to the preservation of Egyptian mummies.

Reading 1

The Story on Food Additives, p. 180

Audio CD 2, Track 4

Warm-up   You may start the lesson in one of the following ways:

*   Bring in—or have the students bring in—some unopened food items. Ask students to read the labels. Then ask them the following questions: What do the labels mean to you? Do you understand the contents? Do you read labels when purchasing food items? Do you assume that food sold with a label is safe?
*   Ask students: What are food additives? Why are they used?

Focus Questions   Write these questions on the board. Ask students to skim the reading passage. Have them discuss, in small groups, what they found.

What are some historical examples of food adulteration?
What are some purposes of food additives?
What are the three unsafe additives discussed? Describe them briefly.

Extension Activity   Play the audio track. Ask students to take notes on the unsafe additives that are discussed in paragraphs 7, 8, and 9. What are they? How are they used and why? What are some of the risks associated with these additives? Play the audio section once or twice more. Have students compare notes with classmates.

Additional Discussion Questions

Do you think vegetarians eat safer foods than meat eaters do? Why or why not?
What are some foods that you think are healthy? Why do you think so?
What is your opinion of the growing focus on organic foods? Why do you think this is happening?

Journal   Write about how the information you have gained from this reading will affect your awareness of the foods that you eat. What changes will you make, if any? Will you shop differently? Are there certain foods that you will add to or subtract from your diet?

Reading 1 Answer Key: The Story on Food Additives

Pre-Reading Activity, p. 179
1. bread   2. ham   3. margarine   4. mayonnaise

Vocabulary, p. 183
1. c   2. b   3. a   4. d   5. b   6. c   7. a   8. d   9. c   10. a

Vocabulary Extension
Part A, p. 185

1. chemicals	**c k**	*Chemicals are added to everything we eat.*
2. pepper	**f g**	*Pepper was adulterated with mustard husks.*
3. tea	**b l**	*Tea was mixed with dried leaves.*
4. candy	**d i**	*Candy was contaminated with copper salts.*
5. saccharin	**a h**	*Saccharin has been linked to cancer.*
6. breakfast cereals	**e j**	*Breakfast cereals are loaded with food dyes.*

Part B, p. 185
Possible answers:
1. What is added to everything we eat?
2. What was adulterated with mustard husks?
3. What was tea mixed with?
4. What was contaminated with copper salts?
5. To what disease has saccharin been linked?
6. What are breakfast cereals loaded with?

Comprehension
Main Ideas, p. 186
1. c   2. d   3. a

Details, p. 186
1. Additives are put into food to make things lighter, tastier (more flavorful), easier to prepare, last longer, look more appetizing, and feel better in our mouths (more pleasing to the palate).
2. Tea was adulterated in 18th-century London because it was brought all the way from China and was very expensive.
3. Artificial gassing tricks the tomato into turning red so that it looks ripe, but it doesn't have the flavor of a ripe tomato.
4. Antioxidants are added to oil-containing foods to prevent the oil from spoiling. Chelating agents stop food from discoloring. Emulsifiers keep oil and water mixed together. Flavor enhancers improve the natural flavor of foods. Thickening agents absorb some of the water present in food and make food thicker. They also keep oils, water, and solids well mixed.
5. In the last sentence of paragraph 6, *these* refers to chemicals that are not safe.
6. NutraSweet is commonly used in diet beverages.
7. The word *its* in paragraph 8, sentence 2, refers to meat.
8. Bacon is a special problem because it is thinly sliced and fried at a high temperature. Nitrate, which is harmless, is quickly changed into the more dangerous nitrite by a chemical reaction that occurs at high temperatures of frying.

9. Dyes are widely used in foods to make them more natural looking and more attractive.
10. Red No. 3 has been banned for some uses because it has caused tumors in rats.

Inferences, p. 187
1. b (or a)   2. a   3. d   4. b

Reading 2   BST and Milk Yield, p. 189   Audio CD 2, Track 5

Warm-up   You may start the lesson in one of the following ways:

- Ask students what their opinion is about using animals to serve the needs of human beings. Here are some examples: Monkeys are experimented on in medical laboratories; chickens are given substances so that they will become fatter for human consumption and so that their eggs will be larger; cows are injected with hormones to increase milk production.
- Ask students what the advantages and disadvantages of being a vegetarian are.

Focus Questions   Write these questions on the board. Ask students to skim the reading passage. Have them discuss, in small groups, what they found.

What is the advantage of injecting BST into cows?
Why is BST used in some countries and not in others?
What are some of the human and animal health issues related to BST?

Extension Activity   Is it acceptable for animals to be experimented with to serve human needs? Prepare for a debate on this topic. Divide the class in half and assign each group a different position to argue. Have each group draw up three arguments to support their position. Then ask each group to present their arguments. At the end of the debate, discuss the strength of the arguments and the effectiveness of the examples used to support the arguments.

Additional Discussion Questions

In the United States it is argued that it would be too difficult to label milk from BST-treated cows. What do you think of this?
Do you think products that have been treated with hormones should be labeled? Why or why not?

Journal   Write about how the information you have gained from this reading affects your opinion about animal experimentation. Are you now more informed on this topic?

CNN.com   Video Activity   You may want to share the following information with students and have them compare supermarkets with food stores in their countries. *Cultural Background:* A supermarket is a large store where you can buy all your food in one place. The supermarket is divided into sections, each with a different type of food. For example, there are sections for meat, fish, fruits and vegetables (produce), dry goods, canned foods, and dairy products. People gather their food in a cart (a small buggy) and pay for all of it at once at the check-out counter.

Have students write what they think "organic" means. Write these words and phrases on the board: *natural, home-made, irradiated, genetically altered, hormones, pesticides, antibiotics, conventional, free range, locally grown, tree-ripened, fresh.* While students watch the video, ask them to classify the words as "organic," "non-organic," or "both." Review the questions and vocabulary before showing the video. (See the video script on page 178.)

 Internet Activity Have students find a food label with ingredients or additives they don't know and then use the Internet to find out what they are and why they are used.

Reading 2 Answer Key: BST and Milk Yield

Vocabulary, p. 192
1. c   2. a   3. gut   4. herds   5. b   6. b
7. veterinary   8. b   9. d   10. assessment

Vocabulary Extension
Part A, p. 193
1. b   long-*lasting*
2. a   insulin-*like*
3. d   high-*yielding*
4. e   antibiotic-*resistant*
5. c   small-*scale*

Part B, p. 194
1. A crop that is resistant to insects is <u>insect-resistant</u>.
2. Something that is like a human is <u>human-like</u>.
3. Farms that have large quantities of land and crops are <u>large-scale</u>.
4. A tradition or custom that has stood for a long time is <u>long-standing</u>.
5. An official with a high rank is <u>high-ranking</u>.

Comprehension
Main Ideas, p. 194
1. b   2. b   3. a   4. a

Details, p. 195
1. One effect of BST is to cause the liver to secrete another substance, the insulin-like growth factor (IGF).
2. A cow produces milk for about 300 days after calving, providing it is milked regularly after the calf is taken away.
3. A cow produces the most milk naturally at about 7–9 weeks after calving.
4. In the 1930s, it was found that injecting cows with BST increased milk production.
5. Cows are injected with BST every 14–28 days after their natural lactation has peaked.
6. BST could improve milk yields by around 10% or more.
7. BST was approved for use in the United States in 1994.
8. Antibiotics are used to treat mastitis in cows.
9. The United States thinks it is too difficult to label milk cartons because the milk comes from so many different sources, some using BST and some not.
10. Small-scale farmers are allowed to label cartons of milk from cows not treated with BST.

Inferences, p. 195
The statements that can be inferred are 1, 2, 3, 4, 5, 9, and 10.

Writing
Writing a Summary, p. 197, Reading 1
Sample:

> According to the article, some food lasts longer and looks and tastes more appealing because of food additives. Additives such as vitamins are beneficial, but people have argued over the negative effects of many food additives for hundreds of years. There are three additives that are known to be unsafe. Artificial drink sweeteners, such as NutraSweet, have been linked to mental problems. Sodium nitrite and sodium nitrate, meat preservatives, are known to be factors in stomach cancer. And many artificial colorings, which are generally cheaper than natural ingredients, are unsafe. One dye has caused allergic reactions, and another has caused tumors in rats. Consumers need to be aware of these risks and learn how to shop and eat safely.

Paraphrasing, p. 197, last paragraph (The debate . . .), Reading 2
Sample:

> Based on an article in the *Catalyst*, the focus of the BST argument is how its use would affect the way farms are organized and whether farmers with only a few animals would benefit. At present, use of BST is not allowed in Europe. However, if the United States became a major exporter of dairy products to Britain, there would probably be a powerful outcry in Britain to end the ban on using BST to treat cows. In that case, farmers in Europe would probably be pressured into discontinuing their BST ban.

Student Essay Follow-Up, p. 199
1. The thesis statement is the following: *There are many side effects related to this popular eating habit, most of which are damaging to our health and personal care.*
2. The writer is considering two effects of eating fast food: not getting the vitamins and minerals necessary to maintain good health and not being able to break the addiction to fast food.
3. The first sentence of paragraph 2 is the topic sentence: *The food sold in most fast food restaurants may not be all that good for us.* This is clearly supported with information about how franchises use food that is not fresh and has many preservatives and a statement about the fast food focus on low prices rather than on food quality.
4. The difficulty of changing the addictive fast food diet is the effect the writer is considering in paragraph 3. The writer gives evidence of this by citing a magazine survey.
5. In the conclusion, the writer restates the thesis statement in other words: *In conclusion, eating fast food is not only an unhealthy habit but also a corrupting one.*

Exercise 1, p. 201
Answers will vary. Encourage students to argue the case as being cause or effect.

Exercise 2, p. 203
1. <u>Ear pain occurs</u> when there is a <u>buildup of fluid and pressure in the middle ear</u>. Often during <u>a cold or an allergy attack</u>, particularly in small children, <u>the ear tube becomes swollen shut, preventing the normal flow of fluid from the middle ear</u>. <u>Fluid begins to accumulate</u>, causing <u>stuffiness and decreased hearing</u>. Sometimes <u>a bacterial infection starts in the fluid</u>, resulting in <u>pain and fever</u>. <u>Ear pain and ear stuffiness</u> can also result from <u>high altitudes</u>, such as when <u>flying in an airplane or driving in the mountains</u>. <u>Swallowing</u> will frequently <u>relieve the pressure in the ear tube</u>.

2. Eating candy can <u>produce acids in the body</u>. <u>Consuming carbohydrates</u> can even produce <u>an alcoholic condition in your body</u>. One of our great orators, William Jennings Bryan, gave <u>speeches nationwide about the bad effects of drinking alcohol</u>, <u>causing more than one person to change his drinking habits</u>. Ironically, Bryan himself <u>died of an alcoholic stomach</u> as a result of <u>eating 13 pancakes with syrup for breakfast</u>. <u>Eating the pancakes</u>, which are full of carbo-hydrates, and the sugary syrup <u>created a kind of alcoholic brew in his stomach</u>. This innocently consumed brew <u>produced alcohol poisoning</u>, which in turn <u>led to his death</u>.

3. <u>Exercise</u> is the central ingredient of good health because it <u>tones the muscles, strengthens the bones, makes the heart and lungs work better</u>, and <u>prevents disease</u>. <u>It increases energy and vitality and gives you a good feeling about yourself</u>. This <u>sense of well-being helps you deal better with stress, eases depression, and aids sleep</u>. There are three kinds of exercises, of which <u>strength-ening</u> is the least important because it <u>builds more bulky muscles</u>, although it <u>increases general strength</u>. *Stretching* exercises <u>keep the muscles loose</u> and are a bit more important than weight-lifting. <u>Stretching before doing other kinds of exercises warms up the muscles</u> and <u>makes them looser and less susceptible to injury</u>. *Aerobic* exercises are the key to fitness because they <u>improve your heart and lungs</u>. Your <u>heart speeds up</u> to <u>pump larger amounts of blood</u>. You <u>breathe more frequently and more deeply</u> to <u>increase the oxygen transfer from the lungs to the blood</u>. As <u>a result of these efforts</u>, <u>the heart becomes larger and stronger</u> and <u>your lungs healthier</u>.

Video Activity, p. 208

1. Answers will vary.
2. *to ban:* to forbid
   to irradiate: to treat with radiation to kill germs or substances that cause diseases
   synthetic: biochemically produced, not organic
3. a. The term *organic* on a food label means that the food has not been irradiated or genetically altered and has not been treated with synthetic fertilizers, antibiotics, or hormones. Most pesticides are banned, too.   b. No, it must be 95% organic. c. Certification means that the products have been grown according to organic standards. They are not necessarily better.   d. Consumers pay 10–50% more for organic products.   e. The new labels make shopping for organic foods easier because they are clearer and more reliable than the old ones.
4. Answers will vary.

Chapter 7 Assessment Answer Key

Reading 1 Vocabulary
1. d   2. b   3. b   4. d   5. b   6. a   7. b   8. b   9. a   10. c

Reading 2 Vocabulary
1. d   2. c   3. a   4. d   5. a   6. b   7. d   8. c   9. b   10. b

Language/Writing
1. T   2. T   3. T   4. F   5. F   6. a. C   b. E   c. E   7. a. E   b. C

Teaching Hints

The readings in this chapter address issues related to the humane treatment of animals. Reading 1 traces the development of animal rights movements throughout the world. Reading 2 is concerned with the challenges of cloning, in particular as it relates to the treatment of the animals involved.

- Did you know that in the 1960s there were 29,000 wild and 11,000 domesticated elephants in Thailand and that 40 years later only 2,000 wild and 3,000 domesticated elephants existed there?
- Did you know that Thailand is home to an elephant hospital? This nonprofit hospital rehabilitates sick elephants. Common elephant injuries result from stepping on landmines or becoming stuck in the mud. Elephants who work for humans often get injured because they are overworked, and sometimes they become addicted to drugs that are fed to them so that they can work harder.

Reading 1 — Animal Rights, p. 211 — Audio CD 2, Track 6

Warm-up   You may start the lesson in one of the following ways:

- Have students look at the picture on p. 209. Bring in—or have students bring in—some pictures of animals. Ask students: What are the animals in the pictures doing? Are they wild or domesticated? Where are they commonly found? Are they serving humans? What are some of the common activities of these animals? What are some other animals you can think of that help humans, and what knowledge do you have of them?
- Ask students: What are some ways in which humans help animals?

Focus Questions   Write these questions on the board. Ask students to skim the reading passage. Have them discuss, in small groups, what they found.

> What is the main issue that affects the animal rights debate?
> Who were Henry Salt and Peter Singer?
> What similarities do some researchers believe exist between humans and animals?
> What is the Compassion in World Farming (CIWF) organization and what has it done?
> Why is Germany mentioned?

Extension Activity   Choose one of the following:

- Do you think that the belief in equality, freedom, and the right to be treated in a certain way applies to animals as well as humans? Prepare for a debate on this topic. Divide the class in half, and assign a position on the question to each group. Then have each group draw up three arguments to support their position. At the end of the debate, discuss the strength of the arguments and the effectiveness of the examples used to support the arguments.

- Divide the class into teams of four to six students. Each team should form a small circle with their chairs, with one chair—the "hot seat"—facing away from the board. One student on each team is in the "hot seat." Write the name of an animal on the board so that everyone except the students in the hot seats can see it. Students in each circle should quickly give the student in their hot seat clues about the animal. The first student in a hot seat to guess the animal wins a point for that team. Then everyone rotates seats, and the game continues with the name of another animal on the board.

Additional Discussion Questions
Animals in zoos and circuses entertain and educate the public. What is your opinion of zoos and circuses? Do you think they provide a useful function? Why or why not? Do you think it is important for children to see zoo animals?

Journal
Animals can be categorized into groups such as pets, wild animals, farm animals, and animals used for medical experimentation. Select one of these groups and discuss the help they give to humans. Do you find this appropriate and necessary?

Reading 1 Answer Key: Animal Rights

Pre-Reading Activity, p. 210
Answers will vary.

Vocabulary, p. 213
1. a   2. a   3. b   4. a   5. c   6. a   7. b   8. c   9. d   10. a

Vocabulary Extension
Part A, p. 214
1. RIGHTS: **human rights.** *Possible answers:* equal rights, inalienable rights, animal rights
2. TREATMENT: **equal treatment.** *Possible answers:* abusive treatment, royal treatment, medical treatment
3. DUTY: **moral duty.** *Possible answers:* familial duty, professional duty, military duty
4. CODE: **moral code.** *Possible answers:* secret code, area code, legal code
5. BEHAVIOR: **human behavior.** *Possible answers:* animal behavior, typical behavior, acceptable behavior

Comprehension
Main Ideas, p. 215
1. Paragraph 3 describes the main issue affecting the debate about animal rights. The issue is whether animals have "certain inalienable rights" that people have, among which are "Life, Liberty, and the pursuit of Happiness."
2. Henry Salt's philosophy was that human beings are not made to eat meat and that we have a moral duty to treat animals "like us."
3. Human rights became universal in 1948 with the U.N. Declaration of Human Rights. In the 1970s, Peter Singer wrote an essay about how animals should be treated just as humans should. He used the term "animal liberation."
4. Some aspects of our treatment of animals that are called into question by animal rights groups are their treatment in captivity and their use in testing products for humans.

Details, p. 216
1. The aims of the RSPCA were to find and punish the people who deliberately harmed animals.
2. Henry Salt's book on animal rights started a discussion on the subject. He believed that humans were not created to eat meat and that they should treat animals as they would other humans. Whether or not people supported Salt's point of view, this book made people start thinking about the topic.
3. Researchers have learned that chimpanzees experience almost every emotion that humans do. Like humans, they use tools, think ahead, and take care of one another. Key genes in humans and chimpanzees are 99.4 percent the same. Researchers also believe that gorillas, whales, and dolphins have many similarities to humans.
4. Germany was the first country to guarantee animal rights in its constitution. The government determines the conditions under which animals can be held in captivity. Animal testing for cosmetics and nonprescription drugs is also controlled. Finally, Germany funds projects that seek alternatives to testing animals.

Inferences, p. 216
1. Since laws protecting animals preceded laws protecting children in Britain, one might infer that animals were being treated cruelly.
2. It can be inferred that the prevention of suffering of animals and eating meat are related because eating meat requires the killing of animals.
3. Based on information in paragraph 6, one could infer that gorillas, whales, and dolphins, as well as the chimpanzees discussed, might be like humans in terms of their emotional and intellectual capacities.

Reading 2   Clone Farm, p. 217   Audio CD 2, Track 7

Warm-up   You may start the lesson in one of the following ways:

- Have students look at the picture on p. 217. Ask students to describe what is happening and describe how they feel about the picture. *Useful vocabulary:* battery farms (farms that raise chickens/eggs), free-range chickens/eggs (chickens that are allowed to roam and are not force fed)
- Play an animal-association game. Write the names of different animals on cards. Divide the class into two to four teams. The object is for students to provide a word they associate with the animal on the card. For example, if the card says *elephant,* a student might offer "wise" or "big." The student who calls out the first associative word gets a point for his or her team.

Focus Questions   Write these questions on the board. Ask students to skim the reading passage. Have them discuss, in small groups, what they found.

How do the goals of the researchers and farmers differ?
What is the difference between a clone and a chimera?
What are Origen's two major challenges?
According to animal welfare groups, what would some of the negative effects of mass production of chickens be?

Extension Activity   Choose one of the following:

- Organize role-playing in groups of four: battery farm owner, free-range chicken owner, customer, animal rights campaigner. Discuss whether it would be a good idea to ban battery farms.

- Split the class in half and assign one half to be representatives of an animal rights organization and the other to be members of the National Institute of Science and Technology. Have each group draw up three arguments to support their position on the mass production of chickens and then hold a debate. At the end of the debate, discuss the strength of the arguments and the effectiveness of the examples used to support the arguments.

Additional Discussion Questions

Do you believe that cloning has more advantages or disadvantages? Discuss your position.

How can human beings make treatment of chickens more humane and yet benefit from the eggs and meat of chickens?

Journal   Discuss your position regarding the cloning of chickens as it is presented in the reading. Write down your arguments and supports for your arguments.

Video Activity   Watch part of the video without any sound. Ask students to describe the conditions in which the chickens live. Then watch the video with sound and compare what it says with what students thought. Review the questions and vocabulary before watching the video again. (See the video script on page 179.)

Internet Activity   Have students look for more information from animal welfare organizations about the cruel treatment of chickens. Some animal welfare organizations are the Humane Society, the International RSPCA (Royal Society for the Prevention of Cruelty to Animals), and the Fund for Animals. Students should bring their findings to class and discuss them with their classmates.

Reading 2 Answer Key: Clone Farm

Vocabulary, p. 219
1. b   2. b   3. a   4. c   5. d   6. a   7. b   8. b   9. a   10. a

Vocabulary Extension
Part A, p. 220

			Possible answers:	
1. c	fund	**research**	*a project*	*education*
2. a	increase	**suffering**	*employment*	*income*
3. e	meet	**demand**	*requirements*	*obligations*
4. b	scale up	**production**	*your lifestyle*	*expectations*
5. d	modify	**machines**	*behavior*	*expenses*

Comprehension
Main Ideas, p. 221

1. a

2. It is desirable to have chickens that are all identical because they grow at the same rate, have the same amount of meat, and taste the same.

3. Animal welfare groups are against mass production of chickens because it increases the suffering of farm birds.

4. The advantages of mass-producing identical chickens are that the birds can be made to be disease-resistant, they can grow quickly and with less food, and farmers can quickly adopt strains that don't carry food-poisoning bacteria. The disadvantages are that many embryos die, more birds go lame because their bone growth cannot keep pace with their muscle growth, and when one bird is vulnerable to a disease it affects all the clones.

Details, p. 221
1. In paragraph 3, line 4, *it* means the prospect of cloning chickens.
2. A chimera is created in a two-step process. First, embryonic stem cells are removed from a freshly laid (before the cells differentiate), fertilized egg. Then these (donor) cells are injected into the embryo of another freshly laid, fertilized, recipient egg.
3. The difference between a chimera and a clone is that a chimera contains cells from both donor and recipient. A clone contains only donor cells.
4. Origen plans to scale up production of genetically engineered chickens by using machines that can inject 50,000 eggs each hour. Embrex Company is trying to upgrade their machines so that the embryo of each egg can be precisely located and the cells, therefore, precisely injected into the embryos. Precision injections will avoid killing the embryos.
5. Origen's first challenge is to create a chimera.
6. The discrepancy is that Origen's web site discusses the process of engineering birds that lay eggs containing medical drugs, yet Origen's spokesperson says that the company is not considering genetic modification.

Inferences, p. 222
1. Some shoppers might hesitate to buy meat from cloned chickens because the chickens have not been raised naturally or because they have been injected with drugs.
2. From the article it can be deduced that chicken farmers are in favor of the process because it would mean higher profits. Farmers are looking for disease-resistant birds that will grow faster on less food.
3. Origen might be unwilling to reveal details of its results because genetic modification might be involved.
4. From the article it can be deduced that chicken in the United States is going to become more and more mass-produced.
5. The article presents a balanced view of the topic by providing information about and stating positions of groups on both sides of the cloning issue. The author's opinion is not given.

Writing
Writing a Summary, p. 223, Reading 1
Sample:
    According to the article, developments in human rights have influenced the debate on whether the human right to equal treatment should extend to animals. One consideration is how similar humans and animals are. Chimpanzees are known to be similar to humans, and researchers believe that other creatures are as well. Compassion in World Farming (CIWF), a British animal welfare group, has influenced the European Union to create a law protecting animals from inhumane treatment. Germany has even stronger protective laws. Humane treatment of animals is a strong movement around the world today.

Paraphrasing, p. 223, last paragraph, Reading 2
Sample:

As Graves reports, although animal welfare groups argue that using technology to mass-produce chickens would be cruel, this procedure could be well-received by consumers. One positive result of mass production would be that farmers could quickly identify the chicken breeds not at risk for *Salmonella* or similar poisonous bacteria and decrease such dangers in the marketplace. However, it is still not known whether consumers would purchase meat from a clone, genetically engineered or not. Nor is it clear whether the FDA will legalize meat and milk from cloned animals.

Student Essay Follow-Up, p. 223
1. The thesis statement, found in paragraph 1, is the following: *However, it is my belief that this does not mean that animals should have the same rights as humans.*
2. The student's argument is against animal rights. The three reasons he gives in the introductory paragraph are that animals are not the same as humans, that we would not be able to eat animals if we gave them the same rights as humans, and that we would not be able to have animals as pets or for entertainment if we gave them the same rights as humans.
3. In the introduction, the student gives three reasons why he is against animal rights. The first two reasons are developed in the first two body paragraphs; however, the third reason is not developed.
4. All the ideas in body paragraph 1 support the student's opinion.
5. In the conclusion, the writer gives a final comment on the topic. He also restates two of the points he made in the introduction: that animals are different from humans and that we could not eat meat if animals had the same rights as humans. The conclusion mentions nothing about pleasure or entertainment, both of which are mentioned in the introduction as supports for his position.

Exercise 1, p. 226
Possible answers:

2. *For*
   a. It leads to cures for diseases.
   b. It determines product safety.

   Against
   a. Animals have feelings.
   b. Animals do not exist for human manipulation.

3. *For*
   a. It will increase food yield.
   b. It will provide consistent taste.

   Against
   a. It will increase animal suffering.
   b. Consumers will not buy unnaturally altered meat and fish products.

4. *For*
   a. Animals have the same right to life as humans.
   b. Animals have feelings.

   Against
   a. Animal products serve the well-being of humans.
   b. Experimentation on animals advances our medical knowledge.

Exercise 2, p. 228
Sentences 2 and 3 do not use a reliable authority. They are very general and offer no facts or statistics to support their claims.

Video Activity, p. 233

1. Answers will vary.
2. *to roost:* to sit, rest
   rafters: boards that support a roof
   to ban: to not allow
   hare-brained: silly, foolish
3. a. fly away   b. 5,500   c. European   d. 300 percent   e. fewer
4. Answers will vary.

Chapter Eight Assessment Answer Key

Reading 1 Vocabulary
1. c   2. b   3. c   4. a   5. b   6. d   7. a   8. c   9. d   10. b

Reading 2 Vocabulary
1. d   2. a   3. b   4. b   5. d   6. d   7. a   8. d   9. c   10. d

Language/Writing
1. T   2. T   3. F   4. F   5. F   6. T   7. F   8. F   9. T   10. F

Teaching Hints

Both readings in this chapter are excerpts from short stories by authors who live in the United States but whose parents are from other cultures. Reading 1 describes the different views that an adult son and his Chinese-born mother have of family. Reading 2 explores the different understandings that a young American boy and a woman from India have of the word *home.*

Did you know that there are generally considered to be five types of households? Which type is the most common in your country? In which countries are the others typical?

1. The nuclear family is made up of parents and their children.
2. The extended family has three or more generations: parents, their married children, and their grandchildren.
3. The joint family household is composed of two generations, but includes more than one married couple and their children. For example, there may be two brothers, their wives, and their children.
4. The polygamous family household consists of one person who has more than one marriage partner, those partners, and the children from all partners.
5. The communal household may take many forms. It can be composed of a mixture of any of the previous household types, married or unmarried people or a combination, with or without children.

Reading 1   ## Winterblossom Garden, p. 236

Audio CD 2, Track 8

Warm-up   You may start the lesson in one of the following ways:

- Have students look at the picture on p. 234. Ask them to describe this woman. What is she doing, wearing, thinking about?
- Divide the class into groups of four or five. Each group should generate a list of words connected with the word *home* and then sort the words into categories, without writing category headings. Have groups look at each other's work and try to guess what the categories are.

Focus Questions   Write these questions on the board. Ask students to skim the reading passage. Have them discuss, in small groups, what they found.

What is the son's reason for visiting his mother? What is her reaction?
Why are the photos important?
How are the son's and his mother's goals different?

Extension Activity   Divide the class into groups of three. Each group should create a skit in which a parent and child are discussing a topic about which they disagree because it reflects a difference in values. For example, the parent might want the child to wear certain clothes, or the child might want to stay out late. Then the parent and child act out the skit for the rest of the class without speaking. The third member of each group is the narrator, who tells the story to the class as it is being acted. After each group is finished, students identify the value that the parent and child disagreed about. After all groups have finished, students vote on the best skit and narration and tell why it was the best.

Additional Discussion Questions

How is food regarded in your home? What is the importance of having a meal together? Who prepares the meal? Who helps (sets the table, cleans up, etc.)? Do you have family photos? Where are they (on the walls of your home, in your wallet, in a photo album)? When do you look at them? Why? Whom do you show them to?

Do you think the mother and son will ever accept each other's differences? Why or why not?

Journal   Write a story about one of your relatives. It can be true or fictional.

Reading 1 Answer Key: Winterblossom Garden

Pre-Reading Activity, p. 235
Answers will vary.

Vocabulary, p. 238
1. c   2. b   3. b   4. a   5. d   6. b   7. d   8. a   9. c   10. b

Vocabulary Extension
Part A, p. 240
1. manage   *run*
2. revive   *bring back*
3. abandon   *leave*
4. stare   *gaze*
5. hold tightly   *clutch*
6. conceal   *hide*

Part B, p. 240
1. Why is his mother <u>clutching</u> a bouquet in the picture?
2. Why doesn't she want to <u>leave</u> his father?
3. What does the son think as he <u>gazes</u> at the wedding picture?
4. Why does the father <u>hide</u> his pinky?
5. What kind of store does his cousin <u>run</u>?
6. What does the mother think will <u>bring back</u> the aunt's ghost?

Comprehension
Understanding the Story, p. 241
1. The sequence of events in the story is as follows: Mother and son are sitting at her kitchen table. She pours tea for them and insists he eat something. She eats a banana. The son tells her of his photography show. She says his pictures would be better and he would be happy if he were married. The son asks why she thinks so. She puts the food away, goes to the sink, and washes the dishes in silence. She takes a cookie tin from the dining room into the living room, opens it, and puts the contents—family photos—on the coffee table. The son sits next to her. She finds a photo of Uncle Lao-Hu and talks about him, mentioning that women cause him confusion because he didn't marry. Uncle Lao-Hu wants the mother to visit him in Hawaii, but the mother's husband—the narrator's father—won't leave the store. The son suggests she go alone, but she won't leave her husband. The

son suggests she do something for herself such as take English lessons, but she says her husband thinks it would be a waste of time. She puts the photos away. The son stands up and looks at his parents' wedding photo over the sofa. He wonders about his parents and if they really love each other and recalls that when he was a child he thought they went to bed dressed in their work clothes.

2. The son tells his mother that he is going to have a photography show.

3. The mother responds by asking if he still takes sad pictures of old buildings.

4. The son wants his mother to visit Uncle Lao-Hu in Hawaii because he wants her to do something for herself.

5. The mother wants her son to get married because she believes it would make him happy.

Interpreting the Story, p. 241

1. The mother values family and marriage, which she shows by showing her son family photos and encouraging him to get married. The son values his career and independence, which he shows by inviting his mother to his show and encouraging her to do something for herself. He isn't sure how he feels about marriage, which he shows in his reaction to her questions about marriage and in his doubts about his own parents' marriage.

2. The blue cookie tin, which contains family photographs, is important to the son and his mother because the photos provide a connection to the family. The son is curious about his extended Asian family. The mother can tell her son stories about the family and emphasize the importance of marriage.

3. The mother's idea of marriage is that it is necessary and expected and that it gives meaning and fulfillment to life. The son believes that he is fulfilled without marriage. He does not equate marriage with happiness.

Understanding the Characters, p. 241

1. The mother sees marriage as happiness and stability. She mentions to her son that he should get married; says that he would take better pictures if he were married; and suggests that, if he doesn't, he may end up like Uncle Lao-Hu, whom she thinks does unwise things.

2. The son values independence and doesn't believe that marriage equals happiness. He wonders why his mother thinks getting married would make him happy. He suggests that his mother be more independent and visit Uncle Lao-Hu or take English lessons. He looks at his parents' wedding photo and doesn't see his mother as happy or fulfilled.

3. Role plays will vary.

Recognizing Style, p. 242

1. The story is told from the son's point of view. He wants us to sympathize with his point of view.

2. a. The teapot symbolizes tradition.

   b. The blue cookie tin symbolizes the importance of family and, by extension, marriage.

   c. The parents' wedding picture symbolizes the son's doubts about marriage.

3. Some examples of similes and metaphors in the story and how they help us understand the characters are as follows:

"My mother looks at me as if I have spoken in Serbo-Croatian." Serbo-Croatian is a foreign language to both of them. When the son asks his mother why she thinks that his getting married would make him happy, he is speaking nonsense to her, like a foreign language.

To the son, taking English lessons is a metaphor for his mother's independence, which her husband rejects.

The wedding picture of the narrator's parents is a metaphor for the uncertainties of marriage and the doubts the narrator has about getting married.

Warm-up   You may start the lesson in one of the following ways:

- Have students look at the photo on p. 243. Ask: What do you think the story will be about? Have them write the first paragraph of the story they envision.
- Have students sit back-to-back with a classmate. One classmate describes his or her living room, specifying directions (for example, "on the left," "in the middle," "under the table") and describing the photos and artwork on the walls or elsewhere in the room. The other classmate draws what is described. Then they change roles. Finally, have students share their drawings and talk about how accurate they are.
- Ask students: When you were a child, how did you help adults with household chores such as cleaning or preparing meals? Do you think it is important for children to perform such chores? Why or why not?

Focus Questions   Write these questions on the board. Ask students to skim the reading passage. Have them discuss, in small groups, what they found.

What is the relationship between Eliot and Mrs. Sen?
What does Mrs. Sen do every day?
Why is Eliot interested in Mrs. Sen's activities?
What are some differences between Eliot's life with Mrs. Sen and his life with his mother?

Extension Activity   Choose one of the following:

- Play the audio track two more times. Have students write down words or phrases they hear that form a picture in their minds. Then ask them to draw a picture of one image they have from the story and share it with their classmates.
- Ask students to think about the different values of "home" that are important to Mrs. Sen and to Eliot's mother and prepare for a debate on this topic. Have half the class take Mrs. Sen's position and the other half take Eliot's mother's position. Each group should prepare three values to support their side's position. After the debate, discuss the strength of the arguments from both sides.

Additional Discussion Questions

What activities, places, and people do you remember from your childhood? Why do you remember them?
Do you think it is important for people to become acquainted with people from other cultures or who are otherwise different from them? Why or why not?
Have you ever had the opportunity to spend time with someone from another culture? If so, how has that affected you?

Journal   Write about a vivid memory you have of your childhood home. Be descriptive.

CNN.com   Video Activity   *Cultural Background:* Sam Wanamaker was an actor in Hollywood, California, until he found out he was going to be banned from the business because of his political views. He moved to England in 1950, where he continued his acting career and became impassioned about restoring the Globe Theatre, the original home to William Shakespeare's plays during the 1500s and 1600s. The new replica of the original theater was important to him, and to London, as a way for the public to experience Shakespeare's theater as it originally was.

Some phrases Shakespeare coined that are still used today include:

It's all Greek to me: I don't understand
to be tongue-tied: to be at a loss for words
I didn't sleep a wink: I couldn't sleep at all
to vanish into thin air: to be lost
to have too much of a good thing: to enjoy something too much

Ask students to make a list of things they already know about Shakespeare. Can they name any modern-day movies or stories that are based on his works? Review the questions and vocabulary before watching the video. (See the video script on page 180.)

 Internet Activity Other authors students may want to research are Julia Alvarez, Maxine Hong Kingston, and Frank McCourt. They may also want to find other English-speaking authors who write about cultural alienation.

Reading 2 Answer Key: Mrs. Sen's

Vocabulary, p. 246
1. c   2. a   3. b   4. b   5. a   6. a   7. a   8. d   9. c   10. b

Vocabulary Extension
Part A, p. 248

Possible answers:

1. e	gather	**shells**	*fruit*	*firewood*
2. d	chop	**vegetables**	*meat*	*wood*
3. a	peel	**a potato**	*an orange*	*the banana*
4. b	raise	**your voice**	*your salary*	*your arms*
5. c	keep down	**the noise**	*your voice*	*the music*

Part B, p. 248
1. Why does Eliot <u>gather shells</u> on the beach?
2. How does Mrs. Sen like to <u>chop vegetables</u>?
3. How does Mrs. Sen <u>peel a potato</u>?
4. What would happen if Mrs. Sen <u>raised her voice</u>?
5. Why would the neighbors ask her to <u>keep down the noise</u>?

Comprehension
Understanding the Story, p. 249
1. Eliot goes to Mrs. Sen's house every day after school because his mother works and the beach house where he lives with his mother is very cold.
2. At Mrs. Sen's house, Eliot sits on the sofa and watches her chop vegetables, talks to her, looks at the newspaper comics, and eats snacks.
3. Mrs. Sen's home is warm, sometimes too warm, whereas Eliot's home is very cold. In Eliot's home it is very quiet, whereas in Mrs. Sen's home she and Eliot talk to each other.

Interpreting the Story, p. 249
1. When Eliot is with his mother, he feels isolated, lonely, and cold.
2. Eliot lives with his mother, who is usually at work or tired. His mother wants the environment quiet and doesn't like to go anywhere.
3. When he is at Mrs. Sen's, Eliot feels engaged. He enjoys watching her chop vegetables with a strange blade; he enjoys listening to her tell stories about her country, India; he enjoys hearing about how close people are in India, because he feels isolated.
4. Eliot is in school. He isn't interested in gathering beach shells any more, but he is old enough to help his mother vacuum the car, to sit still on Mrs. Sen's sofa, and to be interested in her stories. Mrs. Sen gives him popsicles and comics. He may be about 8 or 9.
5. To Eliot, *home* means a quiet and lonely place. Mrs. Sen's memories of home are just the opposite.

Understanding the Characters, p. 249
1. The values that are important to Mrs. Sen are friendship and a sense of community. She likes to spend time with others, share grief and joy, and help other people.
2. The values that are important to Eliot's mother are privacy, distance from other people, and quiet.
3. Mrs. Sen and Eliot's mother would agree that Eliot's well-being and safety are important. They would agree that Eliot is able to help in doing some chores. They would disagree about issues of privacy and quiet and their idea of "home."

Recognizing Style, p. 250
1. The story is told from Eliot's point of view. It is the same as the author's point of view. The point of view becomes apparent because the reader only sees and experiences things as Eliot does. Mrs. Sen's inner thoughts are not revealed.
2. a. The chopping blade symbolizes something traditional to Mrs. Sen and something exotic to Eliot.   b. The car wash symbolizes the intimacy of a small and warm space, the opposite of Eliot's cold and isolated house.   c. The scarlet powder symbolizes something exotic and curious and something permanent that can't be lost.
3. Following are some examples of similes and metaphors in the story and how they help to convey images:

> "The radiators continuously hissed like a pressure cooker" conveys the loud, almost explosive sound of the radiator. It contributes to the warm image of Mrs. Sen's apartment.
> Mrs. Sen's slippers had ". . . soles as flat as cardboard," conveying an extremely flat image.
> The blade was "curved like the prow of a Viking ship," which helps the reader understand that it was a very curved blade. The comparison to a Viking ship also makes the blade seem strong and relentless.

Narrator and Point of View, p. 251
1. *She always manages to find a picture her son has not seen before; suddenly, he discovers he has a relative who is a mortician in Vancouver. He picks up a portrait of Uncle Lao-Hu.* The reader becomes more distant from the son.
2. *I don't mind going to Mrs. Sen's after school. By September the tiny beach house where my mother and I live year-round is already cold; my mother and I have to bring a portable heater along whenever we move from one room to another, and to seal the windows with plastic sheets and a hair dryer.* The story seems much more immediate.

Student Essay Follow-Up, p. 253
1. The thesis statement is the last sentence of paragraph 1: *Both stories use the narrator's point of view to present the reader with multiple viewpoints on the meaning of home, family, and culture.*
2. A similarity in the use of point of view in these two stories is that both are told through the eyes of one major character. A difference is that "Winterblossom Garden" is told in the first person and "Mrs. Sen's" is told in limited third person.
3. An additional point of similarity between the stories is that they both address cultural alienation. Both Mrs. Sen and the mother in "Winterblossom Garden" are having difficulties adjusting to a new culture that does not always share their values. An additional point of difference is the age of the narrators in the two stories. Eliot is very young, while the son in "Winterblossom Garden" is an adult. Their age difference affects the issues that are important to them and the way they see the world around them.

Video Activity, p. 255
1. Famous plays mentioned in the video are *King Lear, Othello,* and *Romeo and Juliet.* Other very famous ones include *Hamlet, A Midsummer Night's Dream, Julius Caesar,* and *The Tempest.* Shakespeare's plays have been translated into many languages and continue to be performed all over the world, in part because his themes are timeless; they include love, jealousy, politics, and family disagreements.
2. *rubbish:* trash or garbage
   glittering: shiny and bright
   rowdy: loud and rude
3. 1. c   2. d   3. e   4. a   5. b
4. Some features of the Globe Theatre not usually found in modern theaters: Most of the audience stands around the stage; the seats are wooden benches; the roof covers only the stage and some of the seats, with the center open to the sky; there are no microphones or sophisticated stage equipment.
5. Answers will vary.

Chapter 9 Assessment Answer Key

Reading 1 Vocabulary
1. c   2. a   3. c   4. c   5. c   6. b   7. c   8. b   9. d   10. d

Reading 2 Vocabulary
1. b   2. c   3. a   4. b   5. d   6. d   7. c   8. a   9. c   10. b

Language/Writing
1. F   2. T   3. T   4. F   5. T   6. T   7. T   8. F   9. F   10. F

Unit One

Chapter One: Writing a Paragraph

Rules	Examples
Use a topic sentence.	*Scientists have shown that there is no scientific basis for a belief in numerology.* (The topic of this sentence is numerology.)
Include a controlling idea in the topic sentence.	The fact that the writer doesn't believe in numerology is the controlling idea.
Supporting sentences develop the topic sentence.	*I was born on Friday the 13th, and I have been lucky all my life.*
The concluding sentence restates the topic sentence in different words or summarizes the main points in the paragraph.	*As you can see, numerology is not a true science.*

Chapter Two: Writing an Essay

Rules	Examples
An essay must have an introduction, a body, and a conclusion.	An essay is at least three paragraphs long.
The introduction contains general statements.	*In the past 25 years, many new breeds of dogs have been developed.*
The introduction must also contain a thesis statement.	*Some breeds of dogs are not suitable for families.*
The body can be one or more paragraphs.	Each body paragraph has a topic sentence, supporting sentences, and sometimes a concluding sentence.
The body supports the thesis statement.	*Very large dogs can accidentally injure small children.*
The conclusion is the last paragraph of an essay.	The conclusion summarizes the main points and restates the thesis in different words.
Transitions or linking words are used to connect paragraphs.	*<u>Another</u> type of dog that has become popular is the pit bull.*

Chapter Three: Writing an Introduction to an Essay

Rules	Examples
The first statement in an introduction is a general statement.	*The New Year is celebrated on January 1 in most countries.*
The general statement is followed by several increasingly specific statements.	*One of the biggest celebrations is in Times Square in New York City. Millions of people gather there, beginning at 9:00 in the evening.*
The thesis statement is often the last sentence in the introduction and gives the controlling ideas for the essay.	*I spent last New Year's Eve in Times Square, and I will never forget the experience!*

Chapter Four: Writing a Conclusion to an Essay

Rules	Examples
The conclusion can summarize the main points of the essay.	*In conclusion, I found the people friendly, the weather bracing, and the entertainment on the giant monitors absolutely amazing. I have never been so close to so many people at the same time in my life.*
You can rewrite the thesis statement from the introduction in different words.	*New Year's Eve in Times Square was unforgettable.*
You can include a final comment or thought on the subject.	*It was great fun, but I don't think I'll ever do it again.*

Chapter Five: Writing an Example Essay

Rules	Examples
Use appropriate transitions to introduce examples.	For the first paragraph: *One example of . . .* For the second paragraph: *Another example of . . .* For the last paragraph: *A final example of . . .*
You can use *e.g.* to show examples.	*I like all kinds of animals, e.g., cats, dogs, and monkeys.*
In the middle of a sentence, use commas before and after *e.g., for example,* and *for instance.*	*People often get nervous when they have to speak in public, for instance, when they have to answer a question in class.*

Chapter Six: Using Examples in an Example Essay

Rules	Examples
Use transition words like *such as* to introduce examples.	*Alternative therapies, such as homeopathy, are not as popular as conventional Western medicine.*
If the information within the commas is nonessential, use commas before and after phrases with *such as*.	*Chronic illnesses, such as headaches, can sometimes be cured by herbal remedies.*
Each body paragraph must contain a clear example.	*For example, herbal medicines are often less expensive than conventional drugs.*
Each body paragraph must have a topic sentence with a controlling idea.	*I think that herbal medicines are the wave of the future.*

Chapter Seven: Creating a Dominant Impression

Rules	Examples
The first topic sentence in a paragraph usually gives the dominant impression.	*My sister's college roommate, Lisa, had the most beautiful eyes I have ever seen.*
To create a dominant impression, choose the most important feature or character trait of a person and emphasize it.	*Although she wasn't really beautiful, I will always remember how soft her eyes were.*
Adjectives help create a dominant impression.	*She had big, dark brown, almond-shaped eyes.*
Details help support the dominant impression.	*When she talked with you, she would look at you without blinking for several minutes at a time.*

Chapter Eight: Organizing a Narrative

Rules	Examples
A narrative follows the natural sequence of events; it puts the events in logical order.	*1. Finished college.* *2. Applied to medical school.* *3. Received a response.*
Time order words and phrases are used at the beginning of sentences in a narrative to emphasize the time sequence.	*First, he finished college. Then he applied to medical school. A few weeks later, he received a response.*
Time order words (except *then*) are followed by a comma.	*Soon afterward, I saw him in the grocery store.*
The conclusion of a narrative tells the end of the story or the result of the events.	*It turned out that he had not only been accepted, but also received a full scholarship.*

Chapter Nine: Comparing and Contrasting

Rules	Examples
Comparisons look at similarities between two things, people, or ideas.	*Coffee is usually served hot. Tea is also usually served hot.*
Contrasts look at differences.	*Americans drink more coffee than tea. In contrast, the British drink more tea than coffee.*
Items to be compared or contrasted must be of the same general class.	Correct: *In the North, tea is always served hot. However, in the South, iced tea is very popular.*
	Incorrect: *In the North, tea is always served hot. However, in the South, people like fried chicken.*
The points you use for support must be the same for both items being compared and contrasted.	Correct: *Tea is served hot in the North because the weather is cold there. Iced tea is popular in the South because the weather is warmer there.*
	Incorrect: *Tea is served hot in the North because the weather is cold there. However, people in the South like iced tea because it's traditional.*
To clarify comparisons and contrasts, you can use a variety of words and phrases to introduce ideas. (See page 117.)	*In Japan, tea is usually drunk plain, whereas in Britain, it is drunk with milk and sugar.*

Chapter Ten: Using Block Organization vs. Point-by-Point Organization

Rules	Examples

With block organization, all the similarities are discussed in one block of paragraphs, followed by all the differences in another block of paragraphs (or the other way around).	*Similarities and Differences Between Coffee and Tea*
	1. Similarities
	  a. Where it is grown
	  b. Who drinks it
	  c. How much it costs
	2. Differences
	  a. Where it is grown
	  b. Who drinks it
	  c. How much it costs

With point-by-point organization, each paragraph contains a discussion of similarities and differences relating to one of the points.	*Similarities and Differences Between Coffee and Tea*
	1. Where it is grown
	  a. Similarities: coffee and tea
	  b. Differences: coffee and tea
	2. Who drinks it
	  a. Similarities: coffee and tea
	  b. Differences: coffee and tea
	3. How much it costs
	  a. Similarities: coffee and tea
	  b. Differences: coffee and tea

To introduce unexpected ideas, you can use an adverbial clause beginning with *although, even though,* or *though* and followed by a comma.	*Although it wasn't very cold, I decided to wear my coat.*

3 · LANGUAGE

Chapter Eleven: Stating Cause and Effect

Rules	Examples
Look at all the possible causes of an effect.	*People who want to extend their lives may benefit from sleeping more, eating less, and increasing the amount of exercise they get.*
Support each cause with a good example.	*Studies show that people who sleep from seven to eight hours a night live longer than people who sleep less.*
State your most important cause last.	*Although sleeping more and eating less are important in increasing longevity, the single most important factor is the amount of exercise you get.*
Use *because* and *as* to introduce reason clauses.	*Exercise is important <u>because</u> it can help keep your weight under control.*

Chapter Twelve: Using Block Organization vs. Chain Organization

Rules	Examples

With block organization, you discuss all the causes in one block of paragraphs and all the effects in another block.	*How to Live Longer*
	1. Causes
	  a. Sleep more
	  b. Eat less
	  c. Exercise
	2. Effects
	  a. Body repairs itself.
	  b. You don't become overweight.
	  c. Muscles become stronger.

With chain organization, each paragraph contains a discussion of a single cause and effect.	*How to Live Longer*
	1. Cause and effect 1
	  a. Cause: Sleep more
	  b. Effect: Body repairs itself.
	2. Cause and effect 2
	  a. Cause: Eat less
	  b. Effect: You don't become overweight.
	3. Cause and effect 3
	  a. Cause: Exercise
	  b. Effect: Muscles become stronger.

To signal causes, you can use structure words or phrases such as *the first reason, the next reason,* and *because* to introduce clauses.	*Because it is so difficult to do, many people don't start an exercise program.*
To signal effects, you can use structure words or phrases such as *the first effect, as a result,* and *consequently* to introduce clauses.	*Linda started exercising. The first effect was that she lost 15 pounds.*
When these structure words are used to introduce a second clause that is the result of the first clause, use a semicolon before the structure words and a comma after them.	*Larry quit smoking; as a result, his lungs cleared and he could breathe better.*

Chapter Thirteen: Writing an Argument Essay

Rules	Examples
An argument essay contains reasons to support the ideas of the writer.	*We must stop environmental pollution in order to keep our children healthy and to make our cities more attractive.*
The writer can use description, comparison and contrast, or cause and effect to illustrate the points in the essay.	Description: *There are 68 hazardous waste sites in California alone.* Comparison and contrast: *Although Massachusetts has 22 hazardous waste sites, neighboring Connecticut has only 13.* Cause and effect: *Because many large manufacturing companies were located in New Jersey over the last 50 years, there are many hazardous waste sites in this state.*
Reasons may be facts or opinions.	Opinion: *Poor air quality is a big problem.* Fact: *In 1986, the air quality in Los Angeles was unacceptable on 88 days.*

Chapter Fourteen: Writing an Argument Essay (continued)

Rules	Examples
A convincing argument requires concrete facts.	*The air quality in Phoenix, Arizona, has improved. In 1987, air quality there was unacceptable on 42 days. In 1996, that figure had dropped to 5 days.*
Avoid phrases such as *They say . . .* and *Authorities agree . . . .*	Avoid: *They say that the closing of several factories helped improve the air quality.*
Do not use a friend or relative as an authority.	Avoid: *My uncle lives in Phoenix, and he says that the use of better emission systems in cars has made the air cleaner.*
All statements that support an argument must be relevant.	*Parents let their children play outside more when the air quality is better.*

Chapter Fifteen: Using Imagery

Rules	Examples
By using colorful words and expressions in comparisons, imagery often makes writing come alive for the reader.	*The room was as dark as a night with no moon or stars.*
A simile uses *like* or *as* to show the similarity between two things.	*Paul Bunyan was as tall as a tree.*
A metaphor compares two things without the use of *like* or *as*.	*The cold water was a slap in the face.*

4 · LANGUAGE

Chapter 1

Essay Organization

Part of essay	Function	What to write
Introduction	Introduces the essay topic	General statement and thesis statement
General statement	Grabs reader's attention	Opinion Quote Anecdote Question
Thesis statement	States topic and central idea of essay	Main topic Divisions of topic How essay is organized
Body paragraph	Supports thesis statement and talks about one aspect of thesis	Reasons Steps in process Advantages/disadvantages Cause and effect Examples Comparison/contrast
Conclusion	Wraps up ideas and ends essay	Thesis restated in another way Main points of essay restated with a final comment

Chapter 2

Process Essay

Process essay: an essay that describes events chronologically, describes a technical process, or tells someone how to do or make something (a "how to" essay).

Type	Example	Organization
Chronological, Historical	The life of Lincoln	1. Thesis statement 2. Paragraphs organized by time periods 3. Time expressions used to indicate time (Example: *During his . . .*)
Technical process	How computers work	1. Thesis statement 2. Paragraphs organized by steps of process 3. Time expressions used to indicate steps
How to	How to make a sandwich	1. Thesis statement 2. Paragraphs organized by steps of process 3. Time expressions used to indicate steps

Chapter 3

Definition Essay

Definition essay: an essay that defines a word or concept through either a literal definition or an extended definition.

Part of essay	Function
Introduction	1. State the term you will define and a literal definition. Example: *Cleanliness is the state of being free from dirt.* or 2. State the term you will define and an extended definition. Example: *In America, clean means not only free of dirt but free of odor as well.*
Thesis	1. Restate the term. 2. Tell how you will define it. 3. State the aspects of the term that you will write about.
Body	1. Develop one aspect of the term in each body paragraph. 2. Support each aspect with clear examples.
Conclusion	1. Summarize the definition. 2. Make a final comment on the term.

Chapter 4

Description

Descriptive essay: an essay that gives a dominant impression and appropriate supporting details.

Characteristics	Examples
1. Makes narration or exposition more interesting	Descriptor (makes subject memorable): They were put in cages *all their lives.*
2. Creates a dominant impression by emphasizing most important characteristic	Vivid language (impacts our feelings): *cold-blooded* Thugs
3. Uses figures of speech	Simile (shows similarity using *as* or *like*): *She is as pretty as a picture.* *He eats like a bird.* Metaphor (shows similarity indirectly): *You are my cup of tea.*

Chapter 5

Classification Essay

Classification essay: an essay that is organized by classifying the subject matter into groups.

Part of Essay	Function	Examples
Introduction	Define a category of classification.	types of pollution
Thesis statement	Include all group members.	air, water, noise
	Use parallel structure (words of the same grammatical form).	*Some causes of air pollution are factories, cars, aerosol products, and deforestation.* (all nouns)
Body	Use transitions to introduce categories show comparison/contrast show examples	*first, next, finally* *unlike, whereas* *typical, one example*

Chapter 6

Comparison-and-Contrast Essay

Comparison: showing how aspects of one item are similar to aspects of another.
Contrast: showing how aspects of one item are different from aspects of another.

Essay Organization

Type	Organization
Block	Each item is discussed in its own block.
Point-by-Point	Similiarities and differences on the same point are discussed together.

Structure Words

	Sentence connectors	Clause connectors	Others
Comparison	similarly likewise also	as just as and	like (+ noun) both . . . and (be) similar to
Contrast	however nevertheless in contrast on the other hand	although even though while whereas	but yet despite (+ noun) in spite of (+ noun)

4 · LANGUAGE

Chapter 7

Cause-and-Effect Essay

Cause-and-effect essay: an essay in which the reasons (the causes) for a situation (the effect) are explored.

Type of essay	Structure	Examples
Cause Analysis: explains multiple causes that lead to one effect	C→ C→E C→	Why do some children have low IQs? malnutrition ⟶ exposure to toxins ⟶ low IQ indifferent parents ⟶
Effect Analysis: explains the multiple effects of one cause	C→E C→E →E	What are the effects of caffeine addiction? ⟶ insomnia caffeine ⟶ restlessness addiction ⟶ high blood pressure
Causal Chain: connects causes and effects in a chain	C ➤ E ➤ C ➤ E	cows get BST ➤ cows get infections ➤ cows get antibiotics ➤ antibiotics get into human milk supply

Chapter 8

Argument Essay

Argument essay: an essay that argues a point by providing evidence in a logical manner.

Part of essay	Function	Examples
Introduction	Give background information State position in thesis statment	It is necessary to use animals for medical experimentation.
Body paragraph 1	Argument 1	Computer or artificial models are not effective enough.
Body paragraph 2	Argument 2 (stronger than 1)	Most medical advances result from animal experimentation.
Body paragraph 3	Argument 3 (strongest)	Scientists don't know enough about living systems, so they must experiment on one.
Body paragraph 4	Refutation	It's true animals may feel pain or die, but we would not be able to make medical advances without experimenting on them.
Conclusion	Restate thesis or summarize Suggest alternative or demand an action	Animal experimentation is necessary for further medical advancements. There needs to be worldwide acceptance of the fact that animals are necessary for human health and progress.

4 · LANGUAGE

4 • LANGUAGE

Narrator	Characteristics
First person	Story told from the narrator's point of view Uses "I" Reader knows only the mind of the narrator Can be used to increase suspense, create empathy with or distance from the narrator
Third-person omniscient	Story told from an "all knowing" point of view Uses "he," "she," "they" Reader knows the minds of all characters No restriction of time and place
Third-person limited	Story told from one character's point of view Uses "he," "she," "they" Reader knows only the mind and experiences of one character Restriction of time and place

adjectives   words, such as *red, tall,* and *interesting,* that describe nouns

argument essay   a persuasive essay that uses description, comparison and contrast, or cause and effect to illustrate its points

block organization   the essay form in which all the similarities between two things are discussed in one block of paragraphs, followed by another block of paragraphs in which all the differences are discussed, or vice versa

body; body paragraphs   the paragraphs in an essay that follow the introductory paragraph and precede the conclusion

brainstorming   gathering ideas on a topic in preparation for writing an essay, often by listing, clustering, or freewriting

cause-and-effect essay   an essay in which the reasons (the causes) for a situation (the effect) are explored

chain organization   the essay form in which each paragraph contains contrasting information or opinions; a cause-and-effect essay with chain organization would explore one cause and its effect in each paragraph, rather than having all the causes together in one block of paragraphs and all the effects in a second block

chronological order   time order, used to describe personal or historical events in the sequence in which they happened

clustering   making a visual plan of the connections among ideas in preparation for writing an essay

colon   a punctuation mark (:) used to introduce a series after a complete sentence or to introduce a quotation

comma   a punctuation mark (,) used to show a break between sense groups within a sentence

comparison   examining the similarities between two or more items

concluding sentence   sentence that comes at the end of a paragraph and summarizes the ideas in the paragraph

conclusion   the last paragraph of an essay, which summarizes the main points in the essay

concrete supporting detail   a statement containing specific information or exact factual details

contrast   examining the differences between two or more items

controlling idea   an idea that limits the content of a paragraph to one aspect of the topic

dash   a line (—) used to show a break in thought or tone

dominant impression   the main effect a person or thing has on our feelings or senses

drafting   writing a first version of an essay

editing   checking an essay to see if it follows the rules for expressing ideas clearly and the rules for grammar, spelling, and punctuation

e.g.   an abbreviation for the Latin words *exempli gratia*, which mean "for example"

essay   a composition of several paragraphs that gives the writer's opinion on a topic

exclamation point   punctuation mark (!) used after interjections, strong commands, and emphatic statements

fact   a statement that is known to be true, such as a statement of specific information

fragment   a dependent phrase that stands alone as if it were a sentence

freewriting   writing freely on a topic without stopping

general statement   a nonspecific statement that introduces the topic of an essay or gives background information on the topic

imagery   comparisons used to provide clear, vivid descriptions

inference   a reader's guess about something that is not directly stated in a reading passage

introduction   the first paragraph of an essay

linking words   transition words; words used to show relationships between sentences or paragraphs

listing   making a list of ideas on a topic in preparation for writing an essay

logical order   a sequence of ideas that is understandable

metaphor   a comparison of two things without the use of *like* or *as*

narrative   a piece of writing that relates a story of events or actions

noun   a word, such as *man, school,* or *car,* that represents a person, place, or thing

opinion   a statement that describes an individual's personal belief

paragraph   a group of sentences that develop one main idea

* **parallel construction**   a sentence structure in which two or more ideas in a series are expressed in the same grammatical form

* **paraphrase**   information put into different words without changing the meaning of the original

period   a punctuation mark (.) used at the end of a statement or after an abbreviation

point-by-point organization   the essay form in which similarities and differences on one point are discussed in each paragraph

point of view   the perspective from which events are reported; first-person point of view uses *I* or *we,* whereas third-person point of view uses *he, she,* or *they*

question mark   a punctuation mark (?) used to indicate that a question is being asked

quotation marks   punctuation marks (" ") used to indicate a direct quotation or the exact words of a speaker

relevant statement   a statement that is logically related to the fact or opinion it supports

restatement   repetition of an original statement using different words

revising   changing the organization or content of an essay and editing the sentences

run-on sentence   two independent clauses written together without any punctuation or with just a comma

semicolon   a punctuation mark (;) used between two independent clauses not joined by one of the connecting words *and, but, for, or, nor, yet, so* or used to separate phrases or clauses in a series if the phrases or clauses contain commas

simile   a comparison in which *like* or *as* is used to show the similarity between two things

structure words   words that signal the type of information that will follow; in a cause-and-effect essay, *because* is a structure word that signals that a cause will follow

* **summary**   the important information from a published work, reduced in amount and put into different words, without changing its meaning; similar to a paraphrase, only shorter

supporting sentence   a sentence that helps expand and support the ideas in the topic sentence

thesis statement   the main idea of an essay; a complete sentence that states an opinion, idea, or belief

time-order words and phrases   words and phrases, such as *next* and *after a while,* that show the order in which events happen

topic sentence   the most important sentence in a paragraph

transitions; transition words   linking words; words used to show relationships between sentences or paragraphs

*Words marked by an asterisk are in Book 4 only.

Unit One	Chapter One: Color Me Pink

Vocabulary
Circle the letter of the best answer.

1. Drinking coffee gives me a lot of _____.
   a. sadness   b. energy   c. wealth   d. envy
2. If you have _____, you have a lot of money.
   a. kindness   b. health   c. wealth   d. attitudes
3. Peace is another word for _____.
   a. symbol   b. luck   c. rage   d. contentment
4. Slow down! I can't keep up with your _____.
   a. pace   b. attitude   c. personality   d. ailment
5. When two things appropriately happen at the same time for no apparent reason, you have a _____.
   a. ceremony   b. coincidence   c. message   d. symbol
6. People with serious _____ often end up in the hospital.
   a. comfort   b. energy   c. ailments   d. independence
7. To _____ someone is to calm him or her.
   a. excite   b. soothe   c. affect   d. treat
8. Different colors represent different _____.
   a. emotional   b. emotions   c. emotionally   d. emotion
9. For some people, green _____ peace.
   a. symbol   b. symbols   c. symbolizes   d. symbolically
10. The study of _____ includes information on how color affects us.
    a. psychological   b. psychologically   c. psychologist   d. psychology

Grammar/Language
Circle the letter of the correct answer.

1. The topic sentence _____.
   a. always contains a conclusion
   b. allows any idea to be discussed in the paragraph
   c. limits the ideas that can be discussed in the paragraph
   d. isn't always the most important sentence in the paragraph
2. The topic _____.
   a. is the subject of the paragraph
   b. is the same as the controlling idea
   c. always comes at the beginning of the paragraph
   d. is the same as the conclusion
3. The controlling idea is _____.
   a. always found in a supporting sentence
   b. always found in the concluding sentence
   c. always found in the topic sentence
   d. never found in the topic sentence
4. Supporting sentences _____.
   a. always come at the beginning of the paragraph
   b. come after the topic sentence
   c. never contain facts and figures
   d. always come at the end of a paragraph

5. The concluding sentence _____.
   a. always contains facts and figures
   b. always comes at the end of a paragraph
   c. always contains the main idea
   d. never comes at the end of a paragraph
6. What is the topic in this sentence?
   People who wear blue may be feeling depressed.
   a. blue
   b. may be feeling depressed
   c. people who wear blue
   d. depressed
7. What is the controlling idea in this sentence?
   The colors we wear show people how we are feeling.
   a. colors
   b. people
   c. the colors we wear
   d. show people how we are feeling
8. Which sentence supports this topic sentence?
   Psychologists sometimes use color to treat patients.
   a. The Luscher color test gives psychologists information about a person's personality.
   b. People who love nature often wear a lot of green.
   c. Yellow is the symbol of luck in Peru.
   d. Colorgenics is the study of the language of color.
9. Which sentence does <u>not</u> support this topic sentence?
   Colors can be used to heal.
   a. We can use color to cause energy to go to certain parts of our bodies.
   b. White light can help to balance the energy in all parts of the body.
   c. Everyone likes some colors and dislikes others.
   d. Yellow can stimulate the mind and create a positive attitude.
10. Which concluding sentence matches this topic sentence?
    People who spend time in a room react to the color of the walls.
    a. Homeowners should always choose paint colors carefully.
    b. When people spend time in a pink room, they may begin to feel lazy.
    c. The color that a room is painted has an effect on how the people in it feel.
    d. The colors we like and dislike say a lot about our personalities.

Essay Question
Write a paragraph describing what you think about a certain color. Tell what effect it has on you and on other people. Explain how and where people might make good use of this color. Give examples from your own life, if possible. Be sure to include a topic sentence, supporting sentences, and a concluding sentence.

Vocabulary
Circle the letter of the best answer.

1. Starting a new business is a difficult _____.
   a. enterprise   b. injury   c. building   d. attitude
2. I forgot to do the last two questions. I _____ them.
   a. soothed   b. continued   c. injured   d. omitted
3. Long-distance runners need _____.
   a. omens   b. misfortune   c. endurance   d. unhappiness
4. The teacher always _____ the even numbers for homework.
   a. takes   b. assigns   c. allows   d. asks
5. Having a car accident is _____.
   a. omitted   b. a misfortune   c. an omen   d. equality
6. The rain _____ all morning. It just wouldn't stop.
   a. transferred   b. persisted   c. started   d. lifted
7. Rain on your birthday is a bad _____.
   a. opportunity   b. injury   c. enterprise   d. omen
8. I'm not at all _____.
   a. superstition   b. superstitions   c. superstitious   d. superstitional
9. I was _____ to get Mr. Green for a teacher.
   a. luck   b. lucky   c. good luck   d. luckiest
10. Many people share a _____ in the power of numbers.
   a. belief   b. beliefs   c. believe   d. believable

Grammar/Language
Circle T if the sentence is true. Circle F if the sentence is false.

1. An introduction contains a general statement and a
   thesis statement.   T   F
2. A thesis statement should be a plain fact.   T   F
3. A thesis statement may list how it will support an opinion.   T   F
4. An essay is several paragraphs long.   T   F
5. The body of an essay can be one or more paragraphs.   T   F
6. This is a thesis statement: *Lucky numbers around the world*   T   F
7. This is a detail: *Five is an unlucky number in Ghana.*   T   F
8. This is a thesis statement: *Colors can affect people's moods.*   T   F
9. This is a detail: *People feel energized by the color red.*   T   F
10. This is a thesis statement: *Different countries have different
    lucky numbers.*   T   F

Essay Question
Write an outline for an essay discussing your opinion of numerology. Use the following format.

  I. Introduction
     Thesis statement: _____
 II. Body
     A. Topic sentence: _____
        1. Support: _____
        2. Support: _____
     B. Topic sentence: _____
        1. Support: _____
        2. Support: _____
III. Conclusion _____

Vocabulary
Circle the letter of the best answer.

1. The children _____ pictures of pumpkins and witches on their Halloween poster.
   a. celebrated   b. cut   c. pasted   d. tied

2. When we were away on vacation, the newspapers _____ in front of the house.
   a. grew   b. piled up   c. read   d. emerged

3. Please tie those newspapers in small _____.
   a. rocks   b. pieces   c. bundles   d. places

4. In spring, the flowers _____ from under the snow.
   a. emerge   b. disappear   c. move   d. close

5. I was so hungry I _____ the food into my mouth.
   a. moved   b. put   c. deposited   d. shoveled

6. The cat ate all the food. She didn't leave a _____.
   a. lot   b. trace   c. dish   d. fish

7. I always _____ my baking pans with aluminum foil so that I can clean them easily.
   a. line   b. remove   c. steam   d. burn

8. Please answer these questions very _____.
   a. care   b. careful   c. carefully   d. caring

9. Different countries have different Thanksgiving _____.
   a. traditional   b. traditions   c. traditionally   d. tradition

10. How does your family _____ birthdays?
    a. celebrate   b. celebrating   c. celebration   d. celebrations

Grammar/Language
Circle the letter of the correct answer.

1. Which sentence is a general statement?
   a. Valentine's Day is on February 14.
   b. Valentine's Day is a popular holiday in the United States.
   c. Valentine's Day was first celebrated in Italy hundreds of years ago.
   d. Valentine's Day is named in honor of Saint Valentine.

2. Which sentence is a general statement?
   a. Stores in the United States do 50 percent of their annual business during December.
   b. Shoppers spend a lot of money on holiday gifts during December.
   c. I received a watch and two ties for Christmas.
   d. I bought my daughter a new TV for Christmas last year.

3. Which sentence is a thesis statement?
   a. The average turkey served at an American Thanksgiving celebration weighs about 15 pounds and costs over $20.00.
   b. Grandparents, aunts, and uncles, along with a few family friends, are usually invited to Thanksgiving celebrations.
   c. To have a successful Thanksgiving celebration, you must have the right food, the right decorations, and the right guest list.
   d. Sometimes little children make Thanksgiving decorations out of apples, which are dressed up to look like little turkeys.

4. If you start the first sentence of a paragraph with the word *first,* what word should the next sentence start with?
   a. Next   b. Before   c. Finally   d. Last

5. The first statement in an introduction should _____.
   a. be a detail   c. be a general statement
   b. be a thesis statement   d. state a subtopic

3 • ASSESSMENT

6. Which sentence is not a thesis statement?
   a. Many unusual holidays are celebrated in South America.
   b. National holidays are an important way of creating unity within a country.
   c. Independence Day is celebrated on July 14 in France.
   d. Americans celebrate Independence Day in many different ways.
7. If you use chronological order, you arrange things according to _____.
   a. where they happened   c. how big they are
   b. how important they are   d. when they happened
8. A thesis statement _____.
   a. is often the last sentence of the introduction
   b. is often the first sentence of the conclusion
   c. never states a subtopic
   d. does not state the method of organization
9. What word or words would you use to begin the last sentence in a paragraph?
   a. The next step   b. First of all   c. Finally   d. Second
10. Which sentence is not a general statement?
    a. Most American families celebrate Thanksgiving.
    b. I like chicken better than turkey.
    c. Many people don't like turkey.
    d. Our Thanksgiving turkey cost $21.95.

Essay Question
Choose a holiday that is celebrated in your home country. Write an introduction to an essay that will tell about the origin of the holiday, why it is popular in your home country, and how it is celebrated there.

3 • ASSESSMENT

Vocabulary
Circle the letter of the best answer.

1. In order to _____ me to do my homework, my parents offered me five dollars for every A I got last semester.
   a. have   b. help   c. incite   d. allow

2. A job as a volunteer in a hospital _____ a career as a doctor.
   a. can be the launching pad for   c. usually happens at the end of
   b. is unrelated to   d. requires more education than

3. You can suggest your own price at _____.
   a. a department store   b. an auction   c. a supermarket   d. a drugstore

4. My older brother encouraged me a lot. He was an important _____.
   a. graduate   b. enemy   c. inspiration   d. description

5. The ice cream cone I had after losing the game was my only _____.
   a. consolation   b. advertisement   c. invitation   d. take-off point

6. You have to play the game a lot to learn the _____ of soccer.
   a. history   b. fundamentals   c. influence   d. excitement

7. The weather here changes all the time. It's _____.
   a. steady   b. unpredictable   c. unsurprising   d. regular

8. I plan to enter the next _____.
   a. compete   b. competes   c. competition   d. competitive

9. I am generally correct in my _____.
   a. predicted   b. predictions   c. predictable   d. predictably

10. All of the contest _____ had to pay a fee.
    a. entrants   b. entry   c. enter   d. entering

Grammar/Language
Circle T if the sentence is true. Circle F if the sentence is false.

1. The conclusion of an essay can restate the thesis in different words.   T   F
2. The conclusion of an essay tells the reader that you have finished the essay.   T   F
3. You can begin your conclusion with the transition word *next*.   T   F
4. The conclusion introduces a new main idea.   T   F
5. You can add a final comment on the topic in the conclusion.   T   F
6. The words *in summary* and *to summarize* mean the same thing.   T   F
7. The conclusion always sums up the main points in the essay.   T   F
8. The conclusion of an essay introduces a new subtopic.   T   F
9. You should begin your conclusion with a transitional signal.   T   F
10. The conclusion always gives additional supporting information about a subtopic.   T   F

Essay Question
Write a conclusion for an essay with the following introduction.

The Bear Dance ceremony is an important event for many Native American tribes. The celebration includes special foods and ceremonies. The purpose of the observance is to ask the Great Spirit for enough food to feed everyone.

Vocabulary
Circle the letter of the best answer.

1. The teacher gave me a stern look. *Stern* here means _____.
   a. unsmiling   b. silly   c. questioning   d. intelligent
2. If someone *ridicules* you, you feel _____.
   a. curious   b. embarrassed   c. happy   d. better
3. My big brother is arrogant about his new house. *Arrogant* here means overly _____.
   a. confused   b. sorry   c. proud   d. dreamy
4. If your boss fired you for no reason, you would feel _____.
   a. prominent   b. brave   c. loyal   d. bitter
5. When a dark cloud in the sky *indicates* rain, it _____ that rain will fall.
   a. asks   b. denies   c. shows   d. pretends
6. My father is a humble man. Humility is a positive character _____.
   a. bulge   b. trait   c. belief   d. activity
7. A *prominent* nose is a _____ nose.
   a. flat   b. small   c. large   d. pointed
8. The company's _____ meant that several people would lose their jobs.
   a. decide   b. deciding   c. decision   d. decided
9. New York City drivers must have a lot of _____
   a. courageous   b. courage   c. courageously   d. courages
10. There is _____ proof that smoking causes cancer.
    a. scientific   b. scientist   c. science   d. scientifically

Grammar/Language
Circle the letter of the correct answer.

1. In an example essay, _____.
   a. the thesis statement comes in the first body paragraph
   b. transitions are never used
   c. there are always three paragraphs
   d. you can use the abbreviation *e.g.* in place of the words *for example*
2. You would use the words *another example of* _____.
   a. in the first body paragraph   c. in the introduction
   b. in the second body paragraph   d. in the conclusion
3. You should not use the words *a final example of* _____.
   a. with your strongest example   c. in the first body paragraph
   b. in the last body paragraph   d. with factual information
4. Before your most important example, use the phrase _____.
   a. the most significant example   c. an additional example
   b. for example   d. for instance
5. The abbreviation *e.g.* means _____.
   a. the most important example   c. an additional example
   b. finally   d. for example
6. Which is a correct sentence?
   a. For example, I don't like ice cream.
   b. For instance, chocolate cake.
   c. For instance, the kind of desserts they have in the cafeteria.
   d. For example, my mother's homemade apple pie.
7. Which sentence is <u>not</u> correctly punctuated?
   a. Fear, for instance, is a strong feeling.
   b. Most strong feelings, for example fear and anger show in the face.
   c. Everyone likes positive feelings, for example, happiness and peace.
   d. Positive feelings, for instance, happiness and peace, are common.

8. Which sentence is correctly punctuated?
    a. I enjoy outdoor sports too, e.g., tennis and swimming.
    b. I enjoy outdoor sports, too, e.g. tennis and swimming.
    c. I enjoy outdoor sports, too, e.g., tennis and swimming.
    d. I enjoy outdoor sports, too e.g., tennis and swimming.
9. Which sentence is <u>not</u> correctly punctuated?
    a. For instance, I like chocolate chip cookies.
    b. For example, not everyone likes dessert.
    c. For instance we had fruit for dessert last night.
    d. For example, I enjoy making pies and cakes on the weekend.
10. Which sentence is correctly punctuated?
    a. I believe for example, that most people's faces reveal a lot about them.
    b. For instance I think that phrenology makes a lot of sense.
    c. Take, for example the idea that faces reflect personality.
    d. Consider, for instance, how many people have large noses.

Essay Question
Write three body paragraphs of an example essay on the topic *Things I like about myself* or *Things I like about my friend* _____. First, outline the examples you are going to give in each paragraph. Then write the paragraphs, using an appropriate transition at the beginning of each one.

Vocabulary
Circle the letter of the best answer.
1. Alternative physicians use nontraditional _____ to heal people.
   a. explanations   b. discussions   c. approaches   d. studies
2. Western medicine is _____ in the United States.
   a. insignificant   b. respected   c. rare   d. ignored
3. The human body's need for food is _____ its need for sleep.
   a. related to   c. independent of
   b. the same as   d. more important than
4. Holistic medicine is generally used _____.
   a. to treat chronic diseases   c. during surgery
   b. to treat victims of car accidents   d. by most Western doctors
5. _____ often arises when two people are angry with each other.
   a. Tension   b. Relaxation   c. Humor   d. Happiness
6. Acupuncture may help _____ a headache.
   a. approach   b. complement   c. respect   d. relieve
7. His fancy new car gives Jim a lot of _____ the neighborhood.
   a. knowledge of   b. business in   c. time in   d. prestige in
8. The _____ of reflexology has not been proven.
   a. effective   b. effecting   c. effectiveness   d. effectively
9. The use of herbs to treat fevers has been very _____.
   a. successfully   b. successes   c. success   d. successful
10. Can you _____ that acupuncture really works?
   a. prove   b. proof   c. proves   d. proving

Grammar/Language
Circle T if the sentence is true. Circle F if the sentence is false.
1. You can introduce an example with the words *such as*.   T   F
2. Put commas around a phrase that begins with *such as* when
   it gives essential information.   T   F
3. In an essay, you should always use the same phrases to introduce
   examples.   T   F
4. You should brainstorm before you organize your ideas.   T   F
5. You should write a rough draft before you do a detailed outline.   T   F
6. Every paragraph in the body of an essay should contain
   a clear example.   T   F
7. The body of the essay contains the thesis statement.   T   F
8. Transition words are used to point out examples.   T   F
9. Each body paragraph needs a controlling idea.   T   F
10. Each paragraph can contain more than one idea.   T   F

Essay Question
Prepare notes for an essay about one type of alternative medical treatment. First, brainstorm a list of ideas about the treatment. Next, work out a thesis statement. Then choose two or three of the best examples from your list and make an outline for the essay.

Vocabulary
Circle the letter of the best answer.

1. _____ is a turning motion.
   a. Standing   b. Dwindling   C. Whirling   D. Contributing
2. A small number of people who have the same beliefs or practices are called _____.
   a. a sect   b. a staff   c. a mainstream group   d. an institution
3. A word that describes people who work hard is _____.
   a. equal   b. lazy   c. industrious   d. intelligent
4. Your *quarters* are where you _____.
   a. work   b. sleep   c. shop   d. attend school
5. When objects are located in a lot of different places, they are _____.
   a. centrally located   b. harmonious   c. celibate   d. scattered
6. If you don't need help from anyone else, you are _____.
   a. self-sufficient   b. angry   c. shy   d. dependent
7. To become smaller is to _____.
   a. dwindle   b. weaken   c. expand   d. give up
8. TV is my favorite _____.
   a. invent   b. invented   c. invention   d. inventive
9. Alice is sometimes _____ to me than she is to herself.
   a. kind   b. kinder   c. kindness   d. kindest
10. My mother _____ a wonderful doll for my little sister.
    a. create   b. creative   c. created   d. creation

Grammar/Language
Circle the letter of the correct answer.

1. Giving the dominant impression has to do with describing _____.
   a. how well a person is able to write
   b. how a person affects our feelings and senses
   c. what language a person speaks
   d. how ambitious a person is
2. Writers create a dominant impression by _____.
   a. describing a lot of different features of the person they are writing about
   b. mentioning only one feature of the person they are describing
   c. not mentioning any features of the person they are describing
   d. emphasizing one important feature of the person they are describing
3. Which of the following adjectives would be used to create a dominant impression?
   a. third   b. forgotten   c. generous   d. ordinary
4. An adjective used to create a dominant impression should be supported by _____.
   a. details   b. general statements   c. nouns   d. a topic sentence
5. The dominant impression is usually introduced in _____.
   a. the conclusion   c. the transition words
   b. chronological order   d. the topic sentence
6. Which sentence does <u>not</u> support this dominant impression: *Tim is industrious.*
   a. He painted his apartment last weekend.   c. He often works overtime.
   b. He takes classes at night.   d. He is often late for work.

7. Which sentence does <u>not</u> support this dominant impression: *Ana is self-sufficient.*
    a. She rarely asks people for help with her homework.
    b. She borrows money from her parents a lot.
    c. She lives by herself.
    d. She has a part-time job to help pay for her education.
8. Which sentence does <u>not</u> support this dominant impression: *Lee is intelligent.*
    a. She gets good grades in school.
    b. A lot of people ask her for help with their homework.
    c. She failed math last semester.
    d. She can speak four languages.
9. Which sentence does <u>not</u> support this dominant impression: *Jon is superstitious.*
    a. He thinks the number 13 is lucky.   c. He never walks under a ladder.
    b. He avoids black cats.   d. He believes in "the evil eye."
10. Which sentence does <u>not</u> support this dominant impression: *Lin is frustrated.*
    a. She has been waiting for an hour.
    b. She looks angry.
    c. She is smiling.
    d. She is tapping her foot on the ground.

Essay Question
Write down the names of two friends or family members. Then write several appropriate descriptive adjectives under each name. Think over each list, and circle one or two adjectives that give the dominant impression. Write two supporting details after each adjective you circled. Then write two paragraphs based on your notes.

Weaving It Together, Book 3 Assessment Questions, © *Heinle*

Vocabulary
Circle the letter of the best answer.

1. A person who studies *agriculture* in college learns about _____.
   a. plants   b. history   c. animals   d. medicine
2. If you *struggle* with learning new vocabulary words, you _____.
   a. like doing it   b. avoid doing it   c. enjoy doing it   d. work hard at it
3. To grow peanuts, you need _____.
   a. glue   b. poison   c. soil   d. cotton
4. When you say you are willing to do something for a friend, you are making
   _____.
   a. a field   b. an orphan   c. a support   d. an offer
5. Farmers couldn't grow cotton because their land was _____.
   a. outstanding   b. worn out   c. admitted   d. discovered
6. In the 1800s, colleges didn't provide _____ for black American
   students.
   a. opportunities   b. agriculture   c. fields   d. factories
7. When you allow people to enter your home, you _____ to your house.
   a. support them   b. praise them   c. admit them   d. wear them out
8. I can't wear this coat anymore. It's _____.
   a. wearing   b. worn out   c. worn up   d. wear out
9. I think the Internet is the greatest _____ of the 20th century.
   a. discovered   b. discovery   c. discover   d. discovering
10. Farmers are always trying out new _____ methods.
    a. agriculturally   b. agriculture   c. agricultural   d. agriculture's

Grammar/Language
Circle the letter of the correct answer.

1. A narrative always includes a series of _____.
   a. adjectives   b. events   c. questions   d. nouns
2. A narrative is organized according to _____.
   a. the order in which things happened   c. the length of each paragraph
   b. the importance of each item   d. the interests of the writer
3. Which time order word means *at the same time?*
   a. soon   b. after a while   c. afterward   d. meanwhile
4. Which time order word means *immediately after this event?*
   a. primarily   b. first   c. next   d. one day
5. Which time order word means *after a long period of time?*
   a. meanwhile   b. eventually   c. soon   d. then
6. Which sentence is correctly punctuated?
   a. First, we visited the library.   c. Afterward we saw the dormitories.
   b. Next we decided to have lunch.   d. Finally we took a look at the pool.
7. Which sentence is correctly punctuated?
   a. After, a while we felt hungry.   c. Meanwhile we sat and waited.
   b. A few minutes later my sister arrived.   d. Finally, she arrived.
8. Which sentence is <u>not</u> correctly punctuated?
   a. First, Lisa applied to college.
   b. After that, she waited for an answer.
   c. After a while she decided she didn't want to go to college.
   d. A few days later, her letter of acceptance arrived.

9. Which sentence is correct?
   a. He wanted to help farmers poor.
   b. He couldn't say no to this golden opportunity.
   c. He wanted to become an instructor agricultural.
   d. He was a man tall.
10. Which sentence is <u>not</u> correct?
    a. He always had grades good.
    b. He soon became rich and famous.
    c. He wanted a big, long car.
    d. His research was always complete and accurate.

Essay Question
Think of someone you know who did something brave, kind, or generous. Tell the story of that person's life and character, using time order words and phrases and descriptions to support your narrative.

Vocabulary
Circle the letter of the best answer.

1. Another way to say that a country has many different types of weather is to say that its climate is _____.
   a. stable   b. warm   c. cool   d. diverse

2. Native Americans introduced settlers to _____ on the cob.
   a. peppers   b. corn   c. fish   d. cheese

3. The foods that your parents teach you how to cook are part of your _____.
   a. intelligence   b. heritage   c. personality   d. appearance

4. A food that has little taste is _____.
   a. bland   b. spicy   c. cooked   d. stuffed

5. When you mix two things together, you _____ them.
   a. hold   b. create   c. blend   d. separate

6. Italy is _____ its wonderful pasta.
   a. stuffed with   b. aware of   c. leading to   d. celebrated for

7. When you leave something in water for a long time, you _____ it.
   a. soak   b. dry   c. staple   d. manufacture

8. We read about ancient cultures in _____ books.
   a. historian   b. histories   c. historical   d. history

9. Before eating meat, you have to _____ it.
   a. cooks   b. cooking   c. cook   d. cooked

10. Immigrants to the United States have been _____ in making soccer a popular sport there.
    a. influence   b. influential   c. influenced   d. influencing

Grammar/Language
Circle the letter of the correct answer.

1. _____ involves looking at the differences between two things, people, or ideas.
   a. Punctuating   b. Supporting   c. Contrasting   d. Comparing

2. When you compare or contrast two things, they must be of the same _____.
   a. importance   b. age   c. size   d. class

3. When the block organization pattern is used for an essay, _____.
   a. only similarities are discussed
   b. all similarities are discussed in one place and all differences in another
   c. similarities and differences are discussed in the same paragraphs
   d. only differences are discussed

4. Which of the following introduces a comparison?
   a. however   b. likewise   c. nevertheless   d. while

5. Which of the following introduces a contrast?
   a. similar to   b. on the contrary   c. just as   d. the same as

6. Which word or words could be used to compare two things?
   a. whereas   b. even though   c. although   d. just as

7. Which word or words could be used to contrast two things?
   a. both . . . and   b. yet   c. not only . . . but also   d. similar to

8. *While* and *whereas* are used to show _____.
   a. that one idea is the opposite of another idea
   b. that two ideas are the same
   c. that the first idea is more important than the second
   d. that the two ideas are unrelated

9. Which sentence has the correct punctuation?
   a. Summer is hot, whereas winter is cold.
   b. Summer is hot, whereas, winter is cold.
   c. Summer is hot whereas, winter is cold.
   d. Summer is hot whereas winter is cold.
10. Which sentence has the correct punctuation?
   a. While pies are popular in New England, they aren't so popular in New Mexico.
   b. While, pies are popular in New England they aren't so popular in New Mexico.
   c. While pies are popular, in New England, they aren't so popular in New Mexico.
   d. While pies are popular, in New England they aren't so popular in New Mexico.

Essay Question
Choose two popular foods. Make a brief block organization outline like the one on page 117, showing the similarities and differences between them. Add some details under each main point. Then write one paragraph comparing the two foods and another paragraph contrasting them. Use some of the comparison and contrast words and phrases suggested on page 117.

Vocabulary
Circle the letter of the best answer.
1. If a ceiling is very low, a tall person will have to _____ .
   a. stretch   b. push   c. whisk   d. stoop
2. If you talk a lot about how good your grades are, you aren't very _____ .
   a. pleased   b. excited   c. humble   d. proud
3. I like the hustle and _____ of big city life.
   a. ceremony   b. stillness   c. bustle   d. ritual
4. Coffee is my favorite _____ .
   a. food   b. beverage   c. medicine   d. entertainment
5. If you are *frantic,* you move _____ .
   a. carefully   b. quickly   c. slowly   d. happily
6. Learning two foreign languages at once is a big _____.
   a. example   b. ceremony   c. performance   d. undertaking
7. I must have the best tea possible _____ the cost.
   a. dignified by   b. taken from   c. regardless of   d. because of
8. Coffee is more _____ than tea in the United States.
   a. popularly   b. popularity   c. popularize   d. popular
9. I like to relax when I eat. I don't like a lot of _____ at dinnertime.
   a. formal   b. formality   c. formally   d. formalize
10. You should thank your host _____ .
    a. politely   b. polite   c. politeness   d. politician

Grammar/Language
Circle T if the sentence is true. Circle F if the sentence is false.
1. With point-by-point organization, all the similarities are discussed in the same part of the essay.   T   F
2. In point-by-point organization, the most important point must always come first.   T   F
3. *Although* and *even though* are used to introduce an unexpected idea.   T   F
4. *Even though* and *though* have different meanings.   T   F
5. *Even though* is used to introduce an adverbial clause.   T   F
6. In point-by-point organization, you don't need to use comparison words.   T   F
7. This sentence is punctuated correctly: *Although I like him, he doesn't like me.*   T   F
8. This sentence is punctuated correctly: *Even though I'm tired I'll go.*   T   F
9. This sentence is punctuated correctly: *Though it's late I'm sure he'll be there.*   T   F
10. This sentence is punctuated correctly: *Even though we're early, the seats are all gone.*   T   F

Essay Question

Make a brief point-by-point outline like the one on page 129, showing the similarities and differences between your favorite foods and your parents' favorite foods. The three main points can be

    I. Our favorite foods
    II. Where we obtain our favorite foods
    III. What we like to drink with our favorite foods.

Include at least one similarity and one difference under each main point. Then write three short paragraphs comparing and contrasting your favorite foods and your parents' favorite foods. Use some of the comparison and contrast words and phrases suggested on page 130.

Vocabulary
Circle the letter of the best answer.
1. The words *he* and *she* always describe people of different _____.
   a. parents   b. genders   c. interests   d. heights
2. Learning to speak a foreign language in just one year is _____.
   a. a great achievement   c. inevitable for most students
   b. an ordinary accomplishment   d. a realistic goal for many people
3. To develop _____ of their surroundings, animals move slowly and look carefully.
   a. fear   b. ignorance   c. hatred   d. awareness
4. When a baby takes his or her first step, the baby's movement is usually very _____.
   a. careful   b. confident   c. sad   d. awkward
5. If you have stopped liking a person, he or she is your _____ friend.
   a. former   b. gender   c. clumsy   d. spinster
6. Friendly, helpful workers have a good _____.
   a. title   b. attitude   c. gender   d. attendant
7. Anna enjoys her role as a teacher. *Role* means _____.
   a. time   b. pay   c. job   d. education
8. We should treat young children _____.
   a. sensitive   b. sensitivity   c. sensitively   d. sensitives
9. Bowing to someone demonstrates your _____ for them.
   a. respect   b. respectful   c. respected   d. respectfully
10. She was not _____ that someone was following her.
    a. aware   b. awareness   c. unaware   d. unawareness

Grammar/Language
Circle T if the sentence is true. Circle F if the sentence is false.
1. In cause and effect essays, the situation is the effect.   T   F
2. The reasons for a situation are the causes.   T   F
3. When planning a cause and effect essay, look at only one or
   two causes.   T   F
4. All effects in a cause and effect essay need supports.   T   F
5. All causes should be accompanied by examples.   T   F
6. Always state your most important cause first.   T   F
7. *Because* and *as* are used to introduce reason clauses.   T   F
8. Always use a comma after a reason if you start the sentence
   with *because* or *as*.   T   F
9. Each body paragraph of a cause and effect essay contains
   a thesis statement.   T   F
10. The conclusion of a cause and effect essay contains a restatement
    of the thesis.   T   F

Essay Question
Write a brief cause and effect essay with four paragraphs. Start by making some notes: Choose a situation (effect) that exists in your life and list five or six reasons for it (causes). Then, after each cause, list some specific examples that support it. Brainstorm as many causes and supports as possible. Choose the three best causes to include in your essay. Put the most important cause last. Use *because* and *as* to introduce some reason clauses.

Vocabulary
Circle the letter of the best answer.

1. When you *eliminate* a food from your diet, you _____ it.
   a. remove   b. change   c. adopt   d. like
2. When a new idea *pops up*, it _____ suddenly.
   a. appears   b. is forgotten   c. disappears   d. comes back
3. When you *borrow* something, you _____.
   a. have strong feelings about it   c. improve it
   b. take it   d. threaten it
4. Leo paid a fine for using his cell phone while driving. A *fine* is _____.
   a. a disagreement   c. a recommendation
   b. a misunderstanding   d. a sum of money
5. A *threatening* letter would make you feel _____.
   a. jealous   b. happy   c. afraid   d. popular
6. When there are dark clouds, rain is inevitable. *Inevitable* means _____.
   a. possible   b. certain   c. impossible   d. not likely
7. Many groups are working to preserve blue whales. *Preserve* means
   _____.
   a. understand   b. enjoy   c. change   d. save
8. I'm not sure that I _____ what you just said.
   a. understood   b. understand   c. understanding   d. misunderstand
9. Some languages are _____, but not written.
   a. speak   b. spoke   c. spoken   d. speaking
10. Fear of flying _____ to cause some airlines to go out of business.
    a. threat   b. threatens   c. threaten   d. threatening

Grammar/Language
Circle T if the sentence is true. Circle F if the sentence is false.

1. With chain organization, each cause and effect pair is discussed
   in a separate paragraph.   T   F
2. If the causes and effects are closely linked, it is better to use
   block organization.   T   F
3. An effect may have several causes.   T   F
4. The words *the first reason* signal a cause.   T   F
5. The words *as a result* signal an effect.   T   F
6. The word *consequently* signals a cause.   T   F
7. *Consequently* means the same as *so*.   T   F
8. This sentence is punctuated correctly: *I'm really tired; therefore
   I'm going to bed.*   T   F
9. This sentence is written correctly: *We didn't study;
   Consequently, we failed the test.*   T   F
10. This sentence is punctuated correctly: *It was raining;
    consequently, the picnic was canceled.*   T   F

Essay Question
Write two paragraphs for a chain essay describing a related pair of causes and effects. Choose a topic you know a lot about. For example,

Why soccer is becoming more popular
Why teens like hip-hop music
Why young people shouldn't start smoking

Outline the information first. Use some cause and effect structure words, such as *the first reason, as a result,* etc., as you write your paragraphs.

Vocabulary
Circle the letter of the best answer.

1. Which word best describes the knowledge animals have that helps them survive in the wild.
   a. ideas   b. fear   c. instinct   d. data

2. When an animal *adapts* to a new environment, it _____ .
   a. changes   b. disappears   c. becomes healthier   d. remains the same

3. When you *conserve* natural resources, you _____ .
   a. destroy them   b. lose them   c. save them   d. remove them

4. Which of the following words describes something no longer in existence?
   a. surviving   b. extinct   c. natural   d. timely

5. If an animal is *confined*, it _____ .
   a. is kept in the wild   c. is endangered
   b. cannot move around freely   d. lives on a natural diet

6. The blue whale is _____ species.
   a. an abnormal   b. a pacing   c. a caged   d. an endangered

7. An *unfounded* theory is a theory that is _____ .
   a. without scientific proof   c. ancient
   b. not yet discovered   d. sensible

8. Putting your hand in a lion's mouth is a _____ business.
   a. risk   b. riskier   c. risking   d. risky

9. I don't find zoos very _____ .
   a. entertain   b. entertainment   c. entertaining   d. entertained

10. Some animals may not _____ a cold winter out of doors.
    a. survival   b. survive   c. surviving   d. survived

Grammar/Language
Circle T if the sentence is true. Circle F if the sentence is false.

1. An argument essay is the same as a persuasive essay.   T   F
2. An argument essay is the same as an example essay.   T   F
3. Argument essays often use chronological organization.   T   F
4. In an argument essay, you can use comparison and contrast organization.   T   F
5. You can use only facts in an argument essay.   T   F
6. "Most animals are unhappy in zoos" is a factual statement.   T   F
7. You might use *in addition* as a transition in an argument essay.   T   F
8. In an essay on how zoos treat animals, a discussion of animal rights is relevant.   T   F
9. In an essay on endangered species, examples of environmental pollution are relevant.   T   F
10. The word *thus* can be used to introduce the conclusion of an argument.   T   F

Essay Question
Write two paragraphs about whether or not it is humane for people to keep dogs and cats as house pets. First, choose a point of view and brainstorm a list of facts and examples to support it. Eliminate any information that is not convincing and relevant to the topic. Use one of the transition words on page 174 to introduce your conclusion.

3 · ASSESSMENT

Vocabulary
Circle the letter of the best answer.
1. Which phrase best describes a weed?
   a. a useless plant   c. a type of vegetable
   b. a GM plant   d. a type of crop
2. Which word describes a chemical that kills plants?
   a. genetically modified   b. substance   c. herbicide   d. resistance
3. If a food is good for you, it has _____ value.
   a. resistant   b. nutritional   c. pesticide   d. drought
4. Some insects are _____.
   a. genes   b. pests   c. cells   d. fertilizers
5. If a plant is *resistant* to a disease, the plant _____.
   a. is destroyed by it   c. is not badly affected by it
   b. is genetically modified by it   d. receives nutritional value from it
6. Corn and wheat are examples of _____.
   a. crops   b. soils   c. bacteria   d. risks
7. The number of people who die from hunger every day may _____ 40,000.
   a. absorb   b. modify   c. increase   d. exceed
8. A small animal that harms crops is _____.
   a. an insecticide   b. insects   c. an insect   d. not an insect
9. Fruits and vegetables are _____ foods.
   a. nutritionally   b. nutritional   c. nutrition   d. nutritious
10. The _____ of crops can be increased by the use of herbicides and insecticides.
    a. produce   b. production   c. product   d. producer

Grammar/Language
Circle T if the sentence is true. Circle F if the sentence is false.
1. To make a convincing argument, you need concrete facts.   T   F
2. Vague references to authority help create a convincing argument.   T   F
3. The phrase "They say . . ." is used to introduce a
   convincing argument.   T   F
4. The phrase "Authorities agree . . ." helps build a convincing
   argument.   T   F
5. In building a convincing argument, you should mention a friend
   or relative.   T   F
6. The letters *e.g.* can be used to introduce an example.   T   F
7. This is a concrete supporting detail: *GM crops were first grown
   in 1980.*   T   F
8. This fact lacks support: *GM foods are dangerous to your health.*   T   F
9. This is a concrete supporting detail: *Herbicides are dangerous.*   T   F
10. This fact lacks support: *A lot of GM crops are grown in Australia.*   T   F

Essay Question
Write two paragraphs stating your opinion of the way food is advertised on TV.
Choose a point of view and brainstorm a list of facts and examples to support it.
Use *for example, for instance,* or *e.g.* to introduce some of your examples.

Vocabulary
Circle the letter of the correct answer.

1. When daylight *fades*, it _____.
   a. becomes brighter   c. suddenly disappears
   b. slowly goes away   d. increases
2. Which of the following can have a *handle?*
   a. a cup   b. a river   c. a dog   d. a book
3. One meaning of the word *course* is_____.
   a. disappear   b. slowly   c. difficult   d. route
4. *Hieroglyphics* is a kind of _____.
   a. valley   b. river   c. poetry   d. writing
5. The opposite of a *valley* is _____.
   a. a nation   b. a hill   c. an ocean   d. a river
6. What could you *wrap around* your finger?
   a. a pencil   b. a ring   c. a piece of string   d. a book
7. Lisa found a way _____ she could leave work early.
   a. when   b. which   c. whereby   d. who
8. A *border* is _____.
   a. a tall mountain   c. a valley
   b. the edge of something   d. the same as a handle
9. What is one type of *effluvia?*
   a. streams and rivers   b. snow   c. rain   d. wind
10. A *remembrance* is the same as a _____.
    a. fear   b. idea   c. thought   d. memory

Grammar/Language
Circle T if the sentence is true. Circle F if the sentence is false.

1. The use of word pictures in poetry is called imagery.	T	F
2. A metaphor uses *like* or *as*.	T	F
3. A simile compares one thing to another.	T	F
4. This sentence contains a simile: *As usual, the river felt cold.*	T	F
5. This sentence contains a metaphor: *Rivers are nature's bloodstream.*	T	F
6. This sentence contains a metaphor: *Mountains are meant to be climbed.*	T	F
7. This sentence contains a simile: *Chemical equations are like hieroglyphics to me.*	T	F
8. This sentence contains a metaphor: *Her eyes are as blue as the sky.*	T	F
9. This sentence contains a metaphor: *His hair is golden wheat.*	T	F
10. This sentence contains a simile: *The valley was like a secret room.*	T	F

Essay Question
Write two paragraphs explaining how poetry is different from prose. Include
examples of metaphors, similes, and images that might be used in a poem.

3 • ASSESSMENT

Vocabulary
Circle the letter of the best answer.

1. If a meal *precedes* a meeting, the meal _____ the meeting.
   a. comes before   c. is served during
   b. comes after   d. is served instead of

2. Which of the following describes a feeling of *envy?*
   a. You want to help someone.   c. You want to get closer to someone.
   b. You want what someone has.   d. You respect someone.

3. If you are afraid of something, you might _____ from it.
   a. draw back   b. give refuge   c. outcast   d. watch

4. A person who speaks *precisely* uses language that is _____.
   a. bold   b. exact   c. jealous   d. polite

5. Which of the following is not part of *audacity?*
   a. confidence   b. strength   c. nervousness   d. bravery

6. Which of the following usually happens when you *stumble?*
   a. You understand something.   c. You close your eyes.
   b. You keep moving quickly.   d. You fall.

7. An *outcast* is _____.
   a. someone who teaches others   c. someone no one likes
   b. someone everyone likes   d. someone who has strong feelings

8. Sometimes babies totter as they walk along. What does *totter* mean?
   a. have both feet on the ground   c. feel angry
   b. move quickly   d. move unsteadily

9. An *honorable* person _____.
   a. doesn't respect others   c. always tells the truth
   b. is never reliable   d. steals money

10. Which of the following is usually connected to *taking refuge?*
    a. being afraid   c. being successful
    b. being happy   d. being audacious

Grammar/Language
Circle the letter of the correct answer.

1. What is a *fable?*
   a. a story that contains animal characters
   b. a story that teaches a lesson
   c. a story that was written a long time ago
   d. a story that makes people laugh

2. *A long time ago, high in the mountains of South America, there existed a place where the sun would shine every day and the sky was always clear.* This sentence provides _____ a story.
   a. the style of   c. the setting for
   b. a character description in   d. the moral of

3. Which of the following could not be a *character* in a fable?
   a. an old man   c. a busy bee
   b. an ancient building   d. a newborn baby

4. Which of the following words describes the *tone* of a story?
   a. rural   b. long   c. humorous   d. worthless

5. *Willy was a tall, slow-moving man who always thought twice before he opened his mouth. Some people said he wasn't very intelligent, but those people hadn't taken the time to get to know him.* Based on this excerpt, what is the writer's opinion of the man?
   a. The writer is afraid of the man.   c. The writer is amused by the man.
   b. The writer is angry at the man.   d. The writer is respectful of the man.

6. Which sentence describes a *setting?*
   a. A hundred people were crowded into the subway car.
   b. He noticed a smiling waiter.
   c. She had a sudden thought.
   d. He gave the child a piece of advice.
7. Which of the following is an example of an *abstract idea?*
   a. truth   b. tree   c. child   d. book
8. The *message* of a story is the same as the _____ of the story.
   a. setting   b. moral   c. main character   d. tone
9. *It was a dark and stormy night. Lisa had wrapped the tiny baby in two layers of blankets, which did little to protect him from the pouring rain and powerful winds.* The words *dark and stormy* describe _____.
   a. an abstract idea   b. a character   c. the setting   d. the message
10. Which of the following is most likely the title of a fable?
    a. *Learning About Literature*   c. *How to Swim*
    b. *The History of Mexico*   d. *The Brave Little Mouse*

Essay Question
Write a short fable that illustrates one of the following morals:

It's better to go slowly than to make mistakes.
Envy leads to sadness.
Wealth doesn't always bring happiness.

Make notes about the setting, characters, actions, and conclusion before you begin writing. Be sure your fable shows clearly what the characters learn by the end, what the reader finds out at the end, and what the main message of the story is.

Chapter 1	Artists

Reading 1 Vocabulary
Circle the letter of the correct answer.

1. The _____ painting hung in a central spot in the art museum.
   a. expelled   b. elaborate   c. keen   d. outgoing
2. The _____ of the crash threw the passengers out of the car.
   a. escapades   b. restraint   c. impact   d. contempt
3. Frida _____ her physical disabilities by becoming outgoing.
   a. compensated for   b. teased   c. adopted   d. identified with
4. The artist _____ a powerful scene of war and passion.
   a. depicted   b. encouraged   c. influenced   d. thrived on
5. The bus accident was a major _____ in Frida's life.
   a. turning point   b. exhibition   c. priority   d. stimulation
6. Frida was an excellent student and _____ the stimulation of school.
   a. belonged to   b. was confined to   c. encouraged   d. thrived on
7. The _____ storm blew houses into the sea.
   a. entire   b. turbulent   c. dedicated   d. radical
8. Although Frida adored her father, she often _____ him.
   a. adopted   b. loved   c. recognized   d. rebelled against
9. The police had been searching for the _____ criminals for years.
   a. intellectual   b. crippling   c. inspirational   d. notorious
10. Despite suffering from a _____ disease, he lived every day to its fullest.
    a. strong   b. bold   c. fatal   d. lively

Reading 2 Vocabulary
Circle the letter of the correct answer.

1. The racer was in front, then fell behind, and then was once again in first place. He _____ the lead.
   a. manipulated   b. influenced   c. reclaimed   d. enabled
2. We need to face this difficult problem. It's necessary to _____ it.
   a. transmit   b. come to grips with   c. form   d. reform
3. I'm looking for an architectural magazine that comes out once a month. Would I find it in the _____ section?
   a. paper   b. periodical   c. territory   d. printer
4. This result was obvious. We should have _____ the outcome.
   a. anticipated   b. manipulated   c. developed   d. retouched
5. The first flowers appear in spring. They generally _____ in April.
   a. duplicate   b. are founded   c. change   d. emerge
6. My favorite musical _____ is jazz. What is your favorite kind?
   a. shape   b. application   c. genre   d. invention
7. Over time, plants may change to fit their environment. It's _____ process.
   a. a binary   b. an evolutionary   c. a revolutionary   d. a linear
8. This is _____ hiring process. It's always done the same way.
   a. a conventional   b. an unconventional   c. a secure   d. an illustrated

9. She is young, but she could become a fine actress someday. She has great
   _____.
   a. technology   b. exposure   c. potential   d. production
10. Something is missing here. We must fill in the_____.
   a. gaps   b. challenges   c. problems   d. systems

Writing/Language
Circle the letter of the correct answer.
1. One way to begin the introductory paragraph of an essay is with _____.
   a. a topic   b. examples   c. an anecdote   d. a thesis statement
2. The function of the general statement is to _____.
   a. grab the reader's attention   c. give an example
   b. state the thesis   d. state the method of development
3. The most important part of the introductory paragraph is the _____.
   a. essay   b. examples   c. anecdote   d. thesis statement
4. The thesis statement is located _____ of the paragraph.
   a. at the beginning   c. in the middle
   b. near the beginning   d. at the end
5. The contents of an introductory paragraph develop from _____.
   a. statement to example   c. general to specific
   b. cause to effect   d. specific to general
6. The method of essay organization is _____ in the introduction.
   a. required   c. sometimes indicated
   b. always indicated   d. never indicated
7. One type of essay development is _____.
   a. comparison and contrast   c. general statement
   b. restatement   d. summary
8. Development of the essay's supporting points occurs in the _____.
   a. introduction   b. body   c. conclusion   d. thesis statement
9. The concluding paragraph includes _____.
   a. a topic   b. examples   c. restatement   d. support
10. The concluding paragraph does not include _____.
   a. a summary   c. a comment on the topic
   b. restatement   d. new information

Essay Question
Read the following introductions. Choose one and write a concluding paragraph for it.
1.   Twentieth-century art movements broke away from traditional art styles
      and techniques. Creating an accurate representation of the world became less
      important than being original. Despite the many branches of 20th-century
      art, all forms seem characterized by expression, abstraction, or fantasy.
      "Expression" emphasizes the artist's emotions; "abstraction" focuses on the
      structure of the work of art; "fantasy" explores the world of imagination.
      These three characteristics are also true of digital art, the art of the 21st
      century.
2.   Diego Rivera, Frida Kahlo's husband, was well known for his murals: large
      paintings on public buildings. The Mexican muralists at the time were influ-
      enced by the Mexican Revolution, which began in 1911, and painted murals
      that expressed their feelings about politics and the social order. Like Frida
      Kahlo, they painted their emotional attitudes toward themselves and their
      world. Artists who are passionately influenced by social and political
      upheavals around them may be more successful artists.

Is it art or mathematics? Cubism is an art movement that was started by Pablo Picasso and Georges Braque in 1907. Cubists were not interested in representing the natural world. They created new ways of producing three-dimensional paintings by using geometrical shapes with straight lines and hard edges. These broken images popular in cubist art suggested a new kind of reality.

1. What is the topic?
2. What is the thesis statement?
3. What device is used to grab the reader's attention?

Reading 1 Vocabulary
Circle the letter of the correct answer.

1. The children _____ their game and were late to dinner.
   a. were without the benefit of   c. conquered
   b. got carried away with   d. adopted

2. This is _____ problem that we must solve.
   a. an altered   b. an ongoing   c. a uniform   d. a liberal

3. The young widow didn't _____ a tear at her husband's funeral.
   a. explain   b. make up   c. shed   d. urge

4. She is _____ about cleanliness. She spends at least an hour a day cleaning the house.
   a. fanatic   b. standard   c. indifferent   d. major

5. The lazy student was _____ his studies and had poor grades.
   a. an exception to   b. a shadow of   c. indifferent to   d. available to

6. The _____ gave millions of dollars for medical improvements in Africa.
   a. spelling reform   b. typesetters   c. fanatic   d. philanthropist

7. The word *brunch* comes from _____ the words *breakfast* and *lunch*.
   a. merging   b. evolving   c. cutting   d. confusing

8. The voters were skeptical of the young politician at the _____ of his career, but he earned their trust.
   a. passage   b. end   c. magnet   d. onset

9. Driving over the speed limit is a punishable _____ in many countries.
   a. version   b. offense   c. mess   d. fascination

10. The storm _____ as it moved up the coast of the country.
    a. gained momentum   c. became aware
    b. popped up   d. went out of fashion

Reading 2 Vocabulary
Circle the letter of the word or phrase that has the same meaning as the underlined word or phrase.

1. The Bengal tiger is <u>an endangered</u> species.
   a. a threatened   b. a series of   c. a surrounded   d. an armed

2. The <u>hub</u> of the city is where the skyscrapers are.
   a. satellite   b. civilization   c. center   d. suburb

3. Many <u>notables</u> appeared at the fund-raising event for the hospital.
   a. thieves   b. animals   c. important people   d. peasants

4. The medical technicians <u>hovered about</u> the injured man.
   a. laughed at   b. moved carefully around   c. dared   d. applied

5. The snowstorm <u>ceased</u> at midnight.
   a. stopped   b. revolved   c. dominated   d. crashed

6. The old custom was <u>revived</u> by the villagers.
   a. murdered   b. shocked   c. resurrected   d. multiplied

7. Do you <u>resemble</u> your mother or your father?
   a. encircle   b. raise   c. like   d. look like

8. After the earthquake, my knees were <u>literally</u> shaking so much that I couldn't walk.
   a. not even   b. badly   c. actually   d. quickly

9. The level of political and economic <u>unrest</u> was shown by the large number of citizens demonstrating against the president.
   a. trade   b. behavior   c. masses   d. dissatisfaction

10. It is not a good idea to walk around here without <u>an escort</u>.
    a. an aristocrat   b. a guard   c. a courtier   d. a cat

Language/ Writing
Indicate whether the statement is true or false by writing T or F on the line.
1. _____ A process essay can be organized by time or by steps.
2. _____ A biography is an example of a process essay.
3. _____ *Chronological order* means "time order."
4. _____ A process essay compares two events.
5. _____ The main steps of the process can be listed in the introduction.
6. _____ *For* indicates the length of time.
7. _____ It isn't always necessary to use time signals in a process essay.
8. _____ The body paragraphs of a chronological essay are divided into major time periods.
9. _____ *During* indicates a period of time from its beginning to the present.
10. _____ *First, second,* and *third* are examples of cardinal numbers.

Essay Question
Choose one of the following topics.
1. Write a process essay on how to make your favorite meal.
2. Write a process essay, using chronological order, about the life of a family member or friend.

Optional Question
Read the following process essay introduction and body. Then answer the five questions.

Johannes Gutenberg

Many people have made powerful contributions to mankind. When such fields as philosophy, the arts, and science are considered, names such as LaoTzu, Michelangelo, and Isaac Newton come to mind. One of the greatest developments of civilization was Johannes Gutenberg's invention of the printing press, which first allowed the public to have access to the written word.

Early work experience provided Gutenberg with knowledge he would later use in building his printing press. Born in Germany around 1400, he worked in a minting factory when he was a young man. Then, from 1438 to 1450, Gutenberg developed his press, using his previous training as the basis for combining metals. His press was made of moveable metal type, revolutionizing printing, which had long depended on the wood blocks used in China.

Gutenberg then put his printing press to work. The first printed book, in 1454, was the Bible. The quality of the printed Bible, which became known as the Gutenberg Bible, was so excellent that it was difficult to tell the difference between it and a handwritten version.

Although Gutenberg's invention had worldwide impact, the final years of his life were not significant. He was a brilliant inventor but a poor businessman. Unable to manage his finances, he lost everything and died without riches in 1468, around the time that printing presses were being established throughout Europe.

1. What is the writer's purpose in this essay?
2. Underline the thesis statement.
3. Put the time signals that are used through each phase of the process in parentheses ( ).
4. Underline the topic sentence in each of the body paragraphs. Are the topic sentences supported?
5. Is the process of development clear?

Reading 1 Vocabulary
Circle the appropriate form of the underlined word to complete the sentence.

1. People in most cultures want to be <u>clean</u>. They value _____.
   a. cleaning   b. cleanliness   c. cleaners   d. cleaned

2. Not all people use <u>soap</u>. The ancient Egyptians used a_____ material made of oils and salt.
   a. soaps   b. soaping   c. soapy   d. soaped

3. Public baths have had a <u>social</u> purpose in many cultures. Members of the _____ can get together.
   a. socialize   b. socializing   c. societal   d. society

4. Public baths have had a <u>social</u> purpose in many cultures. People can get together and _____.
   a. socialize   b. socializing   c. societal   d. society

5. Personal hygiene has been influenced by <u>religion</u> and culture. Many _____ standards have determined the extent and value of personal hygiene.
   a. religious   b. religiously   c. religion   d. religions

6. Personal hygiene has been influenced by religion and <u>culture</u>. Many _____ standards have determined the extent and value of personal hygiene.
   a. culturing   b. cultured   c. culturally   d. cultural

7. In the Middle Ages, commoners didn't generally go to <u>baths</u>. They had little opportunity to _____ .
   a. bath   b. bathe   c. bathing   d. bathers

8. In many cultures, bathing is considered a <u>virtue</u>. Baths have a _____ purpose.
   a. virtual   b. virtuous   c. virtually   d. virtuosity

9. <u>Hygiene</u> has different meanings to different people. What does it mean in your culture to be _____ ?
   a. hygienics   b. a hygienist   c. hygienic   d. hygienically

10. Public baths <u>extend</u> over much of the world. History points out their _____ popularity.
    a. extent   b. extension   c. extensive   d. extensiveness

Reading 2 Vocabulary
Circle the letter of the correct answer.

1. A few parts of the exam were easy, but the _____ exam was very difficult.
   a. active   b. probable   c. bulk of the   d. little

2. The _____ travel season in Hawaii is winter.
   a. symbiotic   b. peak   c. foul   d. extinct

3. Because the hurricane was _____, people left their homes quickly.
   a. occasional   b. imminent   c. minor   d. entertaining

4. The dog's _____ made him an excellent guard dog.
   a. ferocity   b. laziness   c. friendliness   d. food

5. Larger animals often _____ smaller animals for food.
   a. guard against   b. attend to   c. regard   d. prey on

6. The professor's glasses were very thick because of his _____.
   a. myopia   b. face   c. intelligence   d. eyelids

7. He bought _____ sweater because it was soft.
   a. a species   b. a required   c. an inviable   d. a fuzzy

4 · ASSESSMENT

8. Fish that are cleaned must often_____ their behavior so that the cleaners can do their work.
   a. modify   b. line up   c. turn   d. use
9. The experts _____ the value of the diamond at three million dollars.
   a. cleaned   b. performed   c. consumed   d. assessed
10. The flag _____ in the wind.
    a. peaked   b. sang   c. undulated   d. was motionless

Language/Writing
Read the following paragraph. Then indicate whether the 10 statements about the paragraph are true or false by writing T or F on the line.

Although the meaning of "intelligence" is very broad, the term seems to have a connection to ability and knowledge. One frequently thinks of an academic, such as a professor, or an intellectual, such as a philosopher. Is intelligence innate or acquired? Is intelligence exclusively a function of the brain? While there are certainly many kinds of intelligence, this essay will consider three kinds of intelligence other than academic or intellectual intelligence: creative, social, and survival.

1. _____ The topic is the literal definition of "intelligence."
2. _____ The writer gives a literal definition of "intelligence."
3. _____ The thesis statement is the second sentence.
4. _____ The thesis statement states the aspects of the term that will be written about.
5. _____ The first body paragraph will discuss academic and intellectual intelligence.
6. _____ This essay will have a total of five paragraphs.
7. _____ Literal definitions can come from the Internet.
8. _____ People might give different extended definitions.
9. _____ An etymology might illustrate how a word's definition has changed.
10. _____ Definition essays are characterized by time signals.

Essay Question
Choose one of the following topics.
1. Write a definition essay on the concept of family. Illustrate your definition in three or four ways.
2. Write a definition essay on health.

Reading 1 Vocabulary
Circle the letter of the word or phrase that has the same meaning as the underlined word or phrase.

1. A judge must <u>be impartial</u>.
   a. treat all sides equally   c. be responsible
   b. be biased   d. be humanitarian
2. The philanthropist made a generous <u>donation</u> to the fund for needy children.
   a. salary   b. speech   c. contribution   d. effort
3. If you are elected to this position, you will receive a monthly <u>stipend</u>.
   a. salary   b. insurance policy   c. benefit   d. status
4. How are you going to <u>deal with</u> this issue?
   a. believe   b. handle   c. agree with   d. encourage
5. The witness was ordered to <u>give testimony</u> in court.
   a. tell his experience   b. appear   c. give evidence   d. give an opinion
6. I vote, but I don't have a political <u>affiliation</u>.
   a. association   b. belief   c. contribution   d. incident
7. The child tried to <u>live up to</u> her parents' expectations.
   a. achieve   b. defy   c. forget   d. survive
8. Because I have no <u>funds</u>, I turned to my sister for help.
   a. friends   b. security   c. emergencies   d. money
9. The lecturer seemed to speak <u>at random</u>. It was difficult to follow him.
   a. without a plan   b. loudly   c. too softly   d. without intellect
10. This <u>mission</u> might last as long as two years.
    a. course   b. epidemic   c. evaluation   d. project

Reading 2 Vocabulary
Circle the letter of the correct answer.

1. The nurse _____ her duties very professionally.
   a. enjoyed   b. agreed with   c. helped with   d. carried out
2. The commuters _____ home before the storm arrived.
   a. insinuated   c. directed all the moves
   b. hastened   d. looked the other way
3. The thieves tried to _____ the evidence by burying it.
   a. ensnare   b. exploit   c. get rid of   d. hazard
4. A successful _____ persuades innocent people to trust him, and then he tricks them.
   a. babysitter   b. nurse   c. con man   d. policeman
5. The enemy's spy _____ the organization in order to learn their secrets.
   a. infiltrated   b. ensnared   c. proposed   d. lost count of
6. The Taj Mahal in India _____ the memory of the king's beautiful young wife .
   a. took steps to   b. blended in   c. is consecrated to   d. got rid of
7. In the jungle, the larger animals generally _____ the smaller ones.
   a. prey on   b. dump   c. give a hand to   d. are indispensable to
8. The wildfire caused great _____ in the suburbs.
   a. pleasure   b. mayhem   c. wiles   d. devotion
9. The police _____ the party after neighbors complained about the noise.
   a. broke up   b. ensnared   c. enjoyed   d. arrested
10. I can't do this by myself. I need someone to _____.
    a. insinuate   b. call   c. send ahead   d. give a hand

Language/Writing
Indicate whether the statement is true or false by writing T or F on the line.

1. _____ Figures of speech are used to make the descriptions more colorful.
2. _____ A description is a figure of speech.
3. _____ A descriptive essay must include narration.
4. _____ A descriptive essay includes a dominant impression.
5. _____ A dominant impression affects our senses.
6. _____ "As ____ as" is the structure of a metaphor.
7. _____ A simile is a direct comparison.
8. _____ Both similes and metaphors are figures of speech.
9. _____ A descriptive essay has the same basic form as a process essay.
10. _____ Figures of speech make a creative comparison.

Essay Question
Choose one of the following:

1. Write a descriptive essay on a cultural practice that you are familiar with. Use two or three adjectives to give the dominant impression. Include a simile or metaphor in your essay.
2. Write a descriptive essay about a celebration you have recently attended. Use two or three adjectives to give the dominant impression. Include a simile or metaphor in your essay.

Reading 1 Vocabulary
Circle the letter of the word that does not fit correctly.

1. It is common for people to _____ body types.
   a. categorize   b. identify   c. catalog   d. enterprise
2. Many people believe that there is a connection between body type and _____.
   a. relationships   b. temperament   c. character   d. personality
3. Stress may cause your back to become _____.
   a. rigid   b. lean   c. tense   d. stiff
4. The ectomorph is _____.
   a. lean   b. skinny   c. unhealthy   d. thin
5. People who don't often use their hands and arms to gesture when they talk may be _____.
   a. phlegmatic   b. reserved   c. hot-tempered   d. melancholic
6. Everybody has two _____.
   a. arms   b. legs   c. feet   d. torsos
7. Someone who does her work carefully is _____.
   a. concerned with detail   b. meticulous   c. cautious   d. precarious
8. A ballet dancer must be _____.
   a. awkward   b. graceful   c. coordinated   d. flexible
9. The winner had a confident _____.
   a. walk   b. stride   c. stoop   d. step
10. No one wants to spend time with people who are _____.
    a. unkind   b. kind   c. mean   d. unfriendly

Reading 2 Vocabulary
Circle the letter of the correct answer.

1. A social person is not _____.
   a. introverted   b. extraverted   c. friendly   d. carefree
2. The inhibited person's behavior is _____.
   a. reserved   b. free and open   c. sociable   d. outgoing
3. Ample evidence is _____.
   a. unimportant   b. big   c. insufficient   d. enough
4. A subtle problem is _____.
   a. obvious   b. personal   c. hardly noticeable   d. clear
5. A pleasant situation is not _____.
   a. enjoyable   b. aversive   c. optimal   d. comfortable
6. A boring lecture is not _____.
   a. stimulating   b. dull   c. relaxing   d. uninteresting
7. Hans is cautious, not _____.
   a. impulsive   b. thoughtful   c. innocent   d. peaceful
8. One dimension of someone's personality is one _____ of his character.
   a. proposal   b. stimulant   c. vision   d. aspect
9. Hierarchical ordering is not _____ ordering.
   a. clear   b. random   c. acceptable   d. off-base
10. A trait is not a _____.
    a. feature   b. characteristic   c. strategy   d. quality

4 • ASSESSMENT

Circle the letter of the item in each of the following groups that does not belong.
1. Weather conditions: a. stormy b. foggy c. dirty d. humid
2. Natural disasters: a. earthquake b. lightning c. tornado d. tsunami
3. Emotions: a. peacefulness b. anger c. anxiety d. poverty
4. Professions: a. adversary b. cook c. researcher d. musician
5. Hobbies: a. laziness b. stamp collecting c. swimming d. travel

Circle the letter of the item that shows parallel structure.
6. He drives carelessly, nervously, and _____.
   a. fast b. in a hurry c. wonderful d. good
7. Bats are plant eaters, fish eaters, and _____.
   a. dangerous b. fly fast c. sleep during the day d. blood drinkers
8. I like reading and _____.
   a. my dog b. shopping c. to cook d. write
9. My favorite foods are tomatoes, cheese, and _____.
   a. carbohydrates b. wine c. peaches d. vitamins
10. The ill woman felt achy, chilled, and _____.
    a. she was tired b. cough c. had a fever d. feverish

Essay Question
Choose one of the following:
1. Write an essay classifying how you spend your free time into three or four major categories.
2. Write an essay about major types of sports, using a principle of classification.

Optional Question
Cross out the item in each group that does not fit. Then identify the principle of classification for the group. The first one is done for you.

1.	~~Norway~~	Thailand	India	Korea	Asian countries
2.	annually	alternatively	biweekly	monthly	_____
3.	wool	cotton	silk	wood	_____
4.	loving	friendly	warm	narrow	_____
5.	broccoli	lettuce	apples	carrots	_____

Reading 1 Vocabulary
Circle the letter of the correct answer.

1. In many parts of Africa, children's growth is _____ because there is not enough to eat.
   a. exaggerated   b. stunted   c. forbidden   d. dainty

2. The elderly woman's family _____ because she was very ill and could not get out of bed.
   a. curled up   c. waited on her hand and foot
   b. bound her feet   d. waited on her hands and feet

3. It's difficult for me to _____ the music when I'm trying to study.
   a. apply   b. ignore   c. enhance   d. uplift

4. The _____ is not part of the leg.
   a. torso   b. calf   c. thigh   d. knee

5. You will _____ to pass the exam because the testing circumstances were poor.
   a. be condemned   c. get a second chance
   b. undergo a chance   d. be tormented

6. People who _____ the law are often sent to jail.
   a. defy   b. define   c. endure   d. apply

7. The boy's repeated requests to stay out late _____. His parents never granted him permission.
   a. fell on deaf ears   c. were cumbersome
   b. were spared   d. relieved the parents

8. I don't think her story was true. She was just being silly and _____.
   a. serious   b. worried   c. slight   d. foolish

9. The 17th century was the _____ in which women began defining shoe fashion in France.
   a. era   b. trend   c. custom   d. application

10. Is vanity the reason people _____ themselves?
    a. adorn   b. accustom   c. serve   d. keep up with

Reading 2 Vocabulary
Circle the letter of the word that has the opposite meaning of the underlined word or phrase.

1. The <u>lower class</u> lived in the cities.
   a. peasants   b. nomads   c. elite   d. barbarians

2. The thief's disguise made him <u>unnoticeable</u> in the crowd.
   a. binary   b. concealed   c. restricted   d. conspicuous

3. It was considered <u>an outrage</u> when the business moved to another city.
   a. acceptable behavior   c. a ridiculous idea
   b. unacceptable behavior   d. a bad financial decision

4. The typical women of that time were <u>outgoing</u> and not shy.
   a. ridiculous   b. evolved   c. clumsy   d. prudish

5. The politician <u>mildly</u> opposed the proposed tax.
   a. obviously   b. vehemently   c. gradually   d. gently

6. Some groups of people spent their lives crossing deserts or plains, living a <u>nomadic</u> life.
   a. settled   b. adventurous   c. restricted   d. random

7. The unusual island species <u>died out</u> because it was illegally hunted.
   a. collapsed   b. didn't survive   c. was restricted   d. evolved

8. This fashion is <u>associated with men</u>.
   a. feminine   b. masculine   c. predominant   d. coed

9. The people of the time were <u>civilized</u>.
   a. evolved   b. bureaucrats   c. barbaric   d. obedient
10. The <u>immigrants</u> lived in the village.
   a. peasants   b. married people   c. indigenous people   d. newcomers

Language/Writing
Indicate whether the statement is true or false by writing T or F on the line.
1. _____ *While* is an indicator of comparison.
2. _____ Computers could be both compared and contrasted in the same essay.
3. _____ Block organization usually has two body paragraphs.
4. _____ Point-by-point organization is used only when items are compared.
5. _____ *Nevertheless, even though,* and *not only . . . but also* are contrast indicators.

Read the paragraph and then write T or F next to statements 6–10.

The quality of German workmanship is well known throughout the world. The larger German cars are well engineered; similarly, the smaller ones are also high-quality constructions. The driver can expect not only the large German cars but also the small ones to be durable and to last a long time. It is also true that both the larger and the smaller German cars are reliable vehicles. Finally, of course the manufacturers of the larger German cars guarantee their products, just as the manufacturers of the smaller ones do.

6. _____ This is a block paragraph.
7. _____ This is a contrast paragraph.
8. _____ The same aspects of large and small German cars are discussed in this paragraph.
9. _____ All examples support the topic sentence.
10. _____ This paragraph begins with a thesis statement.

Essay Question
Write an essay comparing and contrasting a city with a village, town, or rural area you know or know of. Use three or four bases of comparison.

Reading 1 Vocabulary
Circle the letter of the word that does not fit.

1. I cannot _____ this food.
   a. ingest   b. metabolize   c. taste   d. pose
2. These additives are _____.
   a. harmless   b. beverages   c. toxic   d. banned
3. Remove the _____ from the food.
   a. pesticides   b. palate   c. lumps   d. residue
4. Additives can make food _____.
   a. appetizing   b. last longer   c. tasty   d. stiff
5. Some effects of food additives include _____.
   a. tumors   b. substitutions   c. allergic reactions   d. seizures
6. Food additives can prevent _____.
   a. taste buds   b. discoloration   c. spoilage   d. lumpiness
7. Food additives have been _____ food for centuries.
   a. adulterating   b. tricking   c. contaminating   d. poisoning
8. Many food additives are _____.
   a. preservatives   b. bitter   c. controversial   d. debated
9. Whether food additives pose health risks is _____.
   a. disagreeable   b. debatable   c. controversial   d. arguable
10. Food additives are _____.
    a. artificial   b. synthetic   c. sour   d. loaded with preservatives

Reading 2 Vocabulary
Circle the letter of the word or phrase that has the same meaning as the underlined word or phrase.

1. We haven't started the project yet because of some <u>concerns</u> about it.
   a. satisfaction   b. deadlines   c. business   d. worries
2. The injured man was hurt in the <u>gut</u>.
   a. carton   b. udder   c. stomach   d. saliva
3. The tourists saw <u>herds</u> of elephants on the safari.
   a. groups   b. dairies   c. flows   d. panels
4. I'm not qualified to <u>assess</u> this exam.
   a. inject   b. write   c. digest   d. evaluate
5. The <u>incidence</u> of Type 2 diabetes increased in the United States after World War II.
   a. frequency   b. hormone   c. prescription   d. pesticides
6. The <u>peak</u> travel month in that country is April.
   a. lowest   b. busiest   c. commercial   d. sufficient
7. Rain jackets are <u>resistant to</u> water.
   a. long-lasting to   b. broken down by   c. sensitive to   d. not affected by
8. This information <u>runs counter to</u> what I learned yesterday.
   a. bans   b. agrees with   c. is the opposite of   d. threatens
9. This amount of ground coffee should <u>yield</u> 10 cups.
   a. modify   b. produce   c. reduce   d. cost
10. Where should I <u>insert</u> this thermometer?
    a. remove   b. put in   c. justify   d. consume

Language/Writing
Indicate whether the statement is true or false by writing T or F on the line.
1. _____ There are three basic kinds of cause-and-effect essays.
2. _____ A cause-and-effect essay requires analysis.
3. _____ An effect is a result.
4. _____ A cause has only one effect.
5. _____ A causal chain is commonly used in essays that focus on time lines, such as biographies.

Identify each sentence below as a cause (C) or an effect (E).
6. a. _____ It rained for 24 hours.
   b. _____ People put sandbags along the riverbanks.
   c. _____ The river overflowed.
7. a. _____ Anna was very sick.
   b. _____ Anna stayed home from work.

Essay Quesiton
Write a five-paragraph cause or effect essay. Choose one of the following topics:
1. Causes of Pollution
2. Effects of Lack of Exercise on Young People

Reading 1 Vocabulary
Circle the letter of the correct answer.

1. The airlines often _____ the amount of luggage a passenger can have.
   a. imply   b. refuse   c. restrict   d. deny
2. The driver was not guilty because he didn't _____ run over the dog.
   a. harmlessly   b. deliberately   c. legally   d. unintentionally
3. Not feeding an animal enough food is a form of _____.
   a. responsibility   b. misbehaving   c. abuse   d. adoration
4. Hundreds of policemen were _____ the dangerous criminal.
   a. in pursuit of   b. used to   c. not looking for   d. amused by
5. I wonder when I will be informed of the _____ of my job application.
   a. treatment   b. status   c. question   d. foundation
6. Heavy winds _____ and prevented us from sailing.
   a. didn't exist   b. were not forecast   c. were applied   d. prevailed
7. All humans and animals should be given _____ treatment.
   a. humane   b. human   c. aware   d. undignified
8. The superior athlete was _____ strength, speed, and quickness.
   a. searching for   b. justified with   c. endowed with   d. lacking in
9. The tourist's remark was offensive, but she was not _____ her cultur-ally inappropriate behavior.
   a. at the heart of   b. based on   c. related to   d. conscious of
10. What do you think about the _____ of animal rights?
    a. memory   b. issue   c. answer   d. production

Reading 2 Vocabulary
Circle the letter of the correct answer.

1. The company's profits increased because they _____ their sales.
   a. demanded   b. mass produced   c. put off   d. scaled up
2. The young employee _____ having his own company.
   a. envisaged   b. intended to   c. wanted   d. was tricked by
3. If you _____ a classmate, you can exchange ideas.
   a. don't respect   b. team up with   c. clone   d. have the same traits as
4. The foreign student _____ many cultural characteristics of his host country.
   a. put off   b. adopted   c. was absent from   d. supplied
5. The _____ of technology is quickly changing the world.
   a. victim   b. resistance   c. donor   d. era
6. I look forward to the _____ of studying abroad.
   a. cruelty   b. consideration   c. research   d. prospect
7. _____ dinosaur bones have been uncovered in many places in the world.
   a. Massive   b. Lame   c. Breeding   d. Strains of
8. During the winter, many people _____ the flu and get sick.
   a. welcome   b. keep up with   c. contribute to the   d. are vulnerable to
9. The professor _____ the course so that it more accurately addressed the needs of the students.
   a. decreased   b. gave up   c. modified   d. preferred
10. Children all grow at different _____.
    a. heights   b. schools   c. increases   d. rates

Language/ Writing
Indicate whether the statement is true or false by writing T or F on the line.

1. _____ An argument essay mentions both sides of an argument.
2. _____ A strong argument essay shows familiarity with both sides of the argument.
3. _____ An argument essay devotes equal space to both sides of an argument.
4. _____ A strong argument essay can be developed without facts and statistics.
5. _____ The body paragraphs of an argument essay are ordered from general to specific.
6. _____ The body paragraphs of an argument essay generally are organized in order of importance.
7. _____ The body paragraphs of an argument essay generally are organized from most to least important.
8. _____ The refutation generally follows the introductory paragraph.
9. _____ The refutation in an argument essay can be contained in one paragraph.
10. _____ An argument essay often calls for action in the introductory paragraph.

Essay Question
Choose one of the following topics for an argument essay. Then write a six-paragraph essay.

1. Circus animals are an important source of entertainment and education.
2. The requirement for a zoo must be to provide each animal with an environment similar to its native habitat.
3. Using animal fur for human purposes should be prohibited.

Reading 1 Vocabulary
Circle the letter of the correct answer.

1. People who _____ something think about it all the time.
   a. supply   b. imagine   c. are obsessed with   d. give away
2. It is impossible to _____ a second piece of your delicious pie.
   a. resist   b. afford   c. balance   d. imagine
3. It's important for teachers _____ their classes efficiently.
   a. to talk   b. to stretch   c. to manage   d. to refuse
4. The group wanted to _____ the customs of their ancestors.
   a. associate   b. signify   c. bring back   d. imply
5. She thought the boxes were hidden well, but one _____ from underneath the couch.
   a. scattered   b. hid   c. protruded   d. poured
6. The mother _____ her young child's hand as they crossed the street.
   a. left   b. clutched   c. stretched   d. smiled at
7. The woman _____ the diamond her husband had given her.
   a. shaped   b. married   c. gazed at   d. claimed
8. I never expected to win the trophy. I was _____.
   a. wise   b. stunned   c. not surprised   d. tight
9. He broke his _____ when he slipped on the ice.
   a. gallery   b. bouquet   c. tuxedo   d. pinky
10. The dog's long ears _____ over his face when he sleeps.
    a. touch   b. stand   c. are luminous   d. droop

Reading 2 Vocabulary
Circle the letter of the word or phrase with the same meaning as the underlined word or phrase.

1. The moon is a barren landscape.
   a. a fascinating   b. an empty   c. a foreign   d. a cold
2. The child's clothing was strewn on the floor.
   a. in a pile   b. piled neatly   c. spread around   d. dirty
3. There was a row of people in front of the movie theater.
   a. line   b. circle   c. crowd   d. group
4. The workmen hacked down the small trees and bushes before they painted
   the house.
   a. planted   b. roughly cut down   c. threw away   d. carefully cut down
5. She took an array of clothing on her vacation.
   a. simple   b. expensive   c. a lot of   d. a variety of
6. The artist draped his painting with an old coat.
   a. sewed   b. improved   c. cleaned   d. covered
7. The child was reluctant to go into the water.
   a. too large   b. excited   c. unwilling   d. lifted
8. They detected someone they knew in the crowd.
   a. noticed   b. protected   c. saved   d. didn't see
9. The old man sighed wearily as he sat down on the park bench.
   a. cried softly   c. made a tired sound
   b. laughed loudly   d. made an angry sound
10. The passengers were jostled around in the crowded bus.
    a. seated   b. pushed together   c. smoothly riding   d. arguing

Language/Writing

Indicate whether the statement is true or false by writing T or F on the line.

1. _____ In literature, *point of view* means "opinion."
2. _____ A story can be presented from the point of view of any character.
3. _____ Point of view can alternate between characters.
4. _____ Point of view can not alternate between the author and characters.
5. _____ The first-person narrator tells only the narrator's point of view.
6. _____ It is possible for the reader to dislike or distrust the narrator.
7. _____ The first-person point of view can be used to increase suspense.
8. _____ A third-person narrator must use either "he" or "she."
9. _____ A third-person narrator is restricted to either the narrator's point of view or the points of view of all the characters.
10. _____ An omniscient narration uses "I."

Essay Question

Write an essay on one of the following topics:

1. Compare and contrast the character of Mrs. Sen in "Mrs. Sen's" and the narrator's mother in "Winterblossom Garden."
2. Discuss the symbols of tradition in "Winterblossom Garden."

VIDEO SCRIPTS

BOOK 3

Unit One	Changing Colors

Useful Vocabulary
a dye: a substance used to permanently change the color of something
a pigment: a substance that is mixed with other substances to create a color
ultraviolet (UV) light: a type of light ray produced by the sun
spectrum: the entire range of colors

Reporter: This flower print is about to change color right before your eyes. It's not heat that causes the change; it's light. The dye is made with photochromic, or light-sensitive, pigments, colors that change when exposed to ultraviolet light. This car is painted with photochromic paint. It goes from blue to white if the surface is shaded from the UV rays of the sun.

Manufacturer: What we've done is we've manufactured sixteen different colors that will change throughout the entire spectrum.

Reporter: The molecular structure of the pigments in these fibers is altered by UV light, and colors appear. The same thing is possible with a variety of plastics, as shown here. It's the same process that causes some glasses to darken when exposed to UV light. The dye makers, TCS Industries, say the color possibilities are endless, and there are dozens of potential uses, from toys to military applications.

Manufacturer: This is an adaptive t-shirt. This is before. If you went outside, you'd have greens and grays and things of that nature, something that would move through the jungle as you're moving through the light sources.

Reporter: The process starts with the light-sensitive chemicals. They're mixed with dyes, then shipped out for use in plastics and other products. TCS Industries says some other potential uses for photochromic colors are security measures, like putting small amounts in the pigments in credit cards and, someday, even money.

Unit Two	A New England Clambake

Useful Vocabulary
a clambake: an outdoor party, usually on the beach, where people eat seafood that is cooked by steam on heated rocks with seaweed
corn-on-the-cob: fresh corn that is eaten off the ear
clam chowder: a cream-based soup with clams and potatoes
brownies: a rich, chocolate dessert similar to cake
to cater: to cook and serve food for parties, meetings, or other gatherings
shindig: a social gathering (colloquial)
quahog: a type of clam found in the New England area of the United States

Person: Look at that piece.

Reporter: While they call it a clambake, there's lobster, corn-on-the-cob, potatoes, onions, and mussels on the menu, in addition to clam chowder and clams on the half-shell.

Warner: I mean, you can go out to dinner and get a lobster dinner, but this is an abundance of seafood and it's an abundance of food and everybody says, "Oh, it's going to be too much food." But everybody seems to manage to eat everything, including the brownies for dessert once they tell me they're full.

Reporter: Warner has been catering these shindigs on Nantucket for ten years now.

Warner: No two clambakes are alike.

Reporter: You don't always need a beach at this backyard cooker clambake. Warner sets up huge pots of boiling water and steams everything. Of course, she leaves a few quahogs uncooked for the raw bar.

Woman: Watch the technique.

Man: Does it all cut loose?

Woman: Yup.

Reporter: Then there's the pit bake on the beach.

Man: This is about as deep as it gets.

Reporter: After a pit is dug, the crew sets down rocks, and later adds some seaweed.

Warner: It's a method of cooking that's kind of magical, in that there's no coals cooking. It's the heat of the rocks that cooks the food, not the coals. The coals, you'll see later, we'll take out. The rockweed is the seaweed I use. It is the rockweed that has pockets of water in it, and it's really important in your clambake because that's the main source of moisture.

Unit Three	Yoga for Health

Useful Vocabulary
to combat: to fight
UCLA: University of California, Los Angeles
curriculum: a course of study
a pose: a particular way of holding the body for a specific amount of time
carpal tunnel (syndrome): numbness and pain in the wrist caused by repetitive movements such as typing
a wrist splint: a support for a broken wrist

Reporter: More than ten million Americans now practice yoga, and some doctors are even prescribing it to help combat medical problems. At the UCLA School of Medicine, students now take classes on yoga as part of the curriculum.

Doctor: I hope that this impact will carry through their careers and allow them to have a much more open mind to other ways of treating patients.

Reporter: Most Americans practice Hatha yoga, which consists of a series of gentle poses, breathing, and meditation. Each pose is supposed to stimulate circulation in a certain part of the body and improve the health of muscles and internal organs. Recently, researchers studied yoga and found some positive results. They reported in the *Journal of the American Medical Association* that carpal tunnel patients who practiced yoga did better than those who simply wore wrist splints. Other evidence has shown yoga may be effective in helping to treat diabetes, arthritis, and, of course, stress.

Yoga Expert: The first benefit that you'll notice from any form of good yoga is that there will be a stress reduction. The second thing you'll notice is your concentration will improve.

Unit Four — Harlem Photographer

Useful Vocabulary

Harlem: an African-American neighborhood in New York City, famous in the 60s and 70s for its lively art and culture
titan: a giant; a person who has achieved a lot of power or success
dignitaries: people of high power or rank
off-limits: not allowed or permitted
tickling the ivories: playing the piano (ivories = piano keys)
sweet sixteen party: a party for someone's sixteenth birthday
FDR: Franklin Delano Roosevelt, thirty-second president of the United States
compulsion: an uncontrollable strong need to do something
to suffer a stroke: to have a blocked or broken blood vessel in the brain, which sometimes causes death

Reporter: For six decades, Austin Hansen documented the great figures and grand structures of his chosen community, Harlem. He captured local titans—such as Malcolm X and Adam Clayton Powell, Jr.—and recorded the parade of dignitaries who visited Harlem: Emperor Haile Selassie of Ethiopia, the Queen Mother of England, educator Mary McLeod Bethune, a young Martin Luther King, Jr., organizing a march on Washington. For Hansen, a lifetime's work began with a cardboard camera he got as a child in the Virgin Islands.

Hansen: To see something develop, it was like magic, when I made these little things myself, you know, these little pictures.

Reporter: Hansen immigrated to New York in 1928 at the age of 18. During World War II, he served as a photographer's mate—a job usually off-limits to a black sailor at that time. Back in Harlem, he played drums in a band—and always kept a camera in his bag. He caught the great Count Basie tickling the ivories for the dancing Nicholas brothers . . . singer Eartha Kitt . . . jazzman Dizzy Gillespie. He captured the star quality of a very young Leslie Uggams and recorded future movie idol Billy Dee Williams cutting birthday cake with his twin sister at their sweet sixteen party.

Dinkins: He didn't photograph just the celebrities, he photographed life in what we like to call the village of Harlem.

Reporter: Hansen photographed perhaps the most important event in the life of New York's first African-American mayor, David Dinkins' life—his wedding to wife Joyce in 1953.

Dinkins: She was a beautiful bride.

Reporter: No matter how high his office, Mr. Dinkins says, when it came to posing for Hansen, he stood where he was told.

Dinkins: For Hansen, you would do whatever he wanted. And he could take as long as he wanted because everybody liked him.

Reporter: His eldest son didn't understand his father's long hours in the studio, though, until going to work for him.

Hansen Jr: This was a compulsion. It was his art form, and he pursued it for all that it was worth.

Reporter: Hansen served as historian for a number of Harlem churches: St. Martin's Episcopal, the Cathedral of St. John the Divine, the Abyssinian Baptist Church. And while he kept a full schedule of commissioned jobs, he also snapped news photos: a crowd reading about the death of FDR, a woman and her baby just evicted from their home, baseball greats Roy Campanella and Jackie Robinson at a Boys' Club.

Dodson: Each time that a person of African descent broke another racial barrier, each time they broke another racial barrier, he would capture that person's image.

Reporter: Austin Hansen was last caught on film at the opening two weeks ago of an exhibition of works by noted Harlem photographers. He suffered a stroke that night and died three days later. He once wrote to David Dinkins that "time passes, but love endures." The same could be said of his photographs.

Unit Five	Tortillas Today

Useful Vocabulary
to crave: to want something very badly
pita bread: flat bread, made without yeast, that can be split and filled with meat, salad, etc.
a bagel: a round, thick type of bread roll with a hole in the middle
a staple: a common food in the diet
fajitas: a popular Mexican dish in which cooked meat and vegetables are wrapped in a tortilla
lard: animal fat used for cooking

Reporter: Step behind the scenes and witness the daily bread of California piling high for customers who crave tortillas.

Reporter: So what do we have here?

Tortilla Manufacturer: This is our house brand, which is Anita's.

Reporter: Ooh, they're warm!

Tortilla Manufacturer: Very warm, very warm.

Reporter: This is the way that some people like to buy them.

Tortilla Manufacturer: This is the way we sell them here in Southern California. It has to be fresh, and it has to be delivered at the market every day.

Reporter: And the market demands tons and tons of tortillas today. Rivaling pita bread and the bagel, this year Americans will consume over fifty billion tortillas, and that's not including tortilla chips.

Tortilla Manufacturer: Tortillas continue to be an easy, inexpensive way to have a very nice meal. I think that people are looking for different, easier, more nutritious products out in the marketplace, and tortillas fit that mold.

Reporter: Tortillas, especially corn tortillas, have been a staple of Hispanic households for centuries. Flour tortillas came along when the Spanish brought wheat to the New World. The word *tortilla* comes from the Spanish word *torta,* for round cake. Here's how flour tortillas are made at La Reina.

Tortilla Manufacturer: It's become high-tech. You have production capabilities of fifteen hundred dozens per hour coming off the ovens as opposed to yesterday, when it was maybe sixty or seventy dozens per hour.

Reporter: Some are totally machine-made, others are hand-stretched into shape, requiring deft moves not to touch the 300-degree hot surface.

Tortilla Manufacturer: Okay, here we have the finished product. I want you to notice that all these little burn marks are really the taste buds of the tortilla.

Reporter: So these are fresh-as-you-can-get tortillas.

Tortilla Manufacturer: Fresh as you can get.

Reporter: Flour tortillas come in various sizes and varieties today, including whole wheat tortillas and those especially designed for fajitas. Then it's on to the fat. These two tanks behind me illustrate two important choices in flour tortillas today: those traditionally made with lard, and, relatively new on the market, tortillas made with vegetable oil. Although tortillas made with lard are still the number one choice in Hispanic markets, vegetable oil tortillas are gaining popularity nationwide. So are fat-free tortillas.

Tortilla Manufacturer: And these appeal to the total non-Hispanic market, as well as the Hispanic, but depending upon your health requirements. If you are looking for a nutritious meal, less fat, we make the products that appeal to those.

Reporter: So how much fat does a tortilla have, anyway? Well, they're pretty low to begin with: count one gram of fat for a corn tortilla, and depending on their size, two to three grams of fat for a flour tortilla. What goes inside is up to you.

Unit Six	Computer Faces :-)

Useful Vocabulary

a bulletin board: a place on a web site where people can post messages
off-hand: informal; unprepared
a jest: a joke or funny remark
ironic: actions or words meant to suggest the opposite of what you would expect
frowning: a look of disapproval or sadness; the opposite of a smile
a phenomenon: an unusual thing or event
to take off: to gain popularity quickly

Reporter: If you think these are typing mistakes, you haven't been on a computer bulletin board lately.

Sanderson: The most traditional smiley is formed with a colon, and then a dash, and a right parenthesis. And if you turn your head to the left, you can see that that's a smiley face.

Reporter: Computer smileys began about ten years ago, as more and more computer users started talking to each other by electronic mail, known as e-mail for short. Sometimes the line of type didn't convey quite the right emotional message.

Sanderson: You make an off-hand remark, which if you said it to them in person they would obviously know that it was a jest, but if you type it in and all they see are the words, they may take it very wrong and be very offended.

Reporter: Scott Baumann, a computer scientist at Carnegie-Mellon, is given credit for inventing the electronic smiley.

Baumann: You might type something meant to be ironic, and then you put the smiley face afterward to indicate that it's not meant to be taken totally seriously.

Reporter: The smiley was quickly joined by a frowning face.

Baumann: Or you can say something like that [on screen: "My pay has just been cut."], and you indicate that you're not too happy about it.

Reporter: Soon, the phenomenon took off.

Sanderson: There tends to be a very small set which people actually use as punctuation. The rest are smileys that people have invented because it's such a clever idea that you can make faces sideways using just regular characters you can type on a typewriter.

Reporter: For instance, this is a smiley wearing sunglasses. This one has curly hair. And this one needs a haircut. This is a baseball player smiley. Bozo the Clown as smiley. David Sanderson of the University of Wisconsin is the unofficial archivist of smileys. He has collected almost 700 variations, and inventors of new ones send him their creations. Fans say smileys add an important dimension to conversations when you can't hear a voice or watch gestures and facial expressions. Fallman concedes that a good writer can convey emotion without drawing little faces, but he says that doesn't have much relevance to e-mail exchanges.

Baumann: The problem is that on computer bulletin boards people don't take the time to write very carefully. This is, in some ways, more like conversation than like writing a work of literature.

Reporter: And Sanderson predicts that smileys are here to stay, because people communicating through faceless machines welcome the chance to add an extra touch of humanity.

Unit Seven	Genetically Engineered Crops

Useful Vocabulary
consumption: the act of eating
to track down: to find
bushel: a unit of measure used for large quantities of dry goods
a debacle: a disaster
an allergen: something that causes an allergic reaction
stringent: strict; rigid
moratorium: temporary stoppage

Reporter: Starlink is one of seven crop seeds genetically engineered to resist damaging insects, but because of the potential for allergic reactions in humans the U.S. Environmental Protection Agency approved it for animal consumption only.

EPA Analyst 1: Aventis should never have marketed a corn not approved for human consumption.

Reporter: The prospect that more of the corn could show up in other foods has the Agriculture Department and Aventis, the maker of the seed, trying to track down some nine million bushels or about ten thousand truckloads of the stuff. In a statement, Aventis said, "We are taking every reasonable step to locate all Starlink corn. The company has stopped all sales of Starlink and said it will not renew the seed's registration with the EPA." An official at the agency says there's no hard evidence Starlink poses a health risk, nevertheless . . .

EPA Analyst 2: Knowing everything that we know now, that Aventis was not able to assure that the products were being used according to the registration, we wouldn't register it.

Reporter: Analysts said the Starlink debacle will cost upwards of one hundred million dollars. Starlink is the only genetically modified seed on the market that contains a protein called CRY9C.

Aventis: For most, PT proteins are digested very quickly within human digestive juices, but CRY9C isn't, and that's the reason for concern that it might be an allergen, but there's no evidence that it actually is an allergen.

Reporter: The Starlink incident comes as the EPA decides whether to renew the registrations of other genetically altered seeds. Analysts say renewal is likely, but with more restrictions.

EPA Analyst 3: There will be more heightened testing and heightened labeling, and more stringent requirements as far as the segregating, going forward.

Reporter: Such labeling and testing may be needed to restore consumer confidence in bioengineered crops. Environmentalists are taking it a step further, asking for a moratorium on the seeds until more research can be done into their safety.

Unit Eight	A Poetry Prize

Useful Vocabulary

to toil in obscurity: to work on something without receiving credit for it
a recipient: a person who receives an award, title, or honor
to hold at arm's length: to keep at a distance
inaugural: having to do with an inauguration—a ceremony to induct someone into office
awe: great admiration and respect

Reporter: This is hardly the sort of welcome Susan Mitchell is used to, for she has spent her life toiling in obscurity in that most rarified field of writing. Susan Mitchell, you see, is a poet.

Mitchell: The last thing I ever thought of in all the years I've been writing poetry was that anything I wrote was going to make a lot of money.

Reporter: But now she's made a lot of money—fifty thousand dollars, to be exact—as recipient of the Kingsley-Tufts Poetry Award, presented at the Clairmont Graduate School. Her winning entry: a book of verse, titled simply *Rapture*. This, from *Rapture*:

Mitchell: The saddest songs are sung at sunset, and I stir the ice in my drink and let it go, remember, and let it go, which is what the wind does with everything I love . . .

Reporter: Poetry has always had its loyalists, its lovers, but some have always held it at arm's length, even perhaps feared it. That's changing.

Maya Angelou: Lift up your eyes upon this day, breaking for you, give birth again to the dream . . .

Reporter: Maya Angelou's inaugural poem soared and inspired, but more and more young people, it seems, have needed little inspiration as they crowd coffee houses to perform their own works. You may love it, you may hate it, but it seems there's no stopping it.

Poetry Professor: We need all of our poets. We need not just the poets who win prizes, we need those poets who are also writing in obscurity, because they're helping forge the future of our language.

Reporter: Mitchell, a professor at Florida Atlantic University, seems touched at the reawakened interest.

Mitchell: I think perhaps it's happening because American life right now shuts out so many emotions. If you live at the speed of facts, a lot of emotional experiences become impossible: mystery, wonder, awe, love.

Reporter: She will not live in a world without those experiences, and so she will return to her work, a little richer perhaps, a little less obscure perhaps, but still a poet.

| Chapter 1 | Jackson Pollock, Modern Artist |

Useful Vocabulary
daunting: intimidating
colossal: huge
unbridled: chaotic
a canvas: a piece of cloth used as a surface for painting
irreverent: not showing respect

Reporter: The 105 paintings at the Museum of Modern Art are impressive, daunting, breathtaking, and colossal, a testament to the unbridled creativity of a man who felt the desperate need in his life to create. But more than likely this thought runs through your mind at least once when you see a Jackson Pollock painting: "It's just splattered paint! I could have done that." In fact, that may be one of the greatest contributions of Pollock: the notion that art and expression can be owned by anyone.

Curator: The kind of rebellion that we find on the canvas, the kinds of dismissals of certain traditions and opening up of new possibilities is not one that's, I think, accompanied by torment—it's a supreme sense of confidence in himself in a different life lived on the canvas.

Reporter: In the 1940s, when he developed his technique, it became clear there was a method to his madness: a canvas lay on the floor, industrial paint applied straight from the can. But with his irreverent style came controversy. In 1949, *Time Magazine* dubbed Pollock "Jack the Dripper." But no one can argue that it was Pollock who first put modern American art on the international art scene. Fifty years later, Pollock's work still stands out in American art and is drawing huge crowds.

Museum Visitor 1: I think when you see them in person what's amazing is how beautiful they actually are.

Museum Visitor 2: I think the mood is expressed by the color. There's obviously a lot more to it than just splashing a lot of paint around.

Museum Visitor 3: It's an expression of his thinking, of his thought. And I find it really, really impressive. It's very sad in the end, extremely sad.

Reporter: The end for Pollock did come much too soon. At forty-four, a drunken Pollock crashed his car into a tree in 1956. His energetic, emotional, and controversial style endures now forever only on the canvas.

Useful Vocabulary

a tomb: a grave or chamber where a body is buried

hieroglyphics: an ancient system of writing that uses pictorial characters

to decipher: to figure out or interpret the meaning of

Rosetta Stone: a stone discovered by a French soldier in Egypt in 1799. The stone was carved with the same message in three different scripts: Egyptian hieroglyphs, a later form of ancient Egyptian, and Greek. It is now in the British Museum.

posthumous: after someone's death

Coptic: Egyptian Christian

pharaoh: ruler of ancient Egypt

Reporter: The tombs are mute, but the controversy is vocal. Most archaeologists today contend that while we can read hieroglyphics, the sound of the Egyptian language has been lost forever.

Man 1: If an ancient Egyptian were to walk in the door today, we could write messages to each other and communicate very well. But if he were to speak to us or we were to speak to him, I don't think we'd understand a single word.

Man 2: The one who is ruled by the King, the one who is honored under the great God . . .

Reporter: Archaeologists have been able to read the hieroglyphic writing of the ancient Egyptians since 1822, when a French code breaker was able to decipher the text of the famed Rosetta Stone. The ability to read has given us detailed insight into Egyptian lives. For instance, archaeologists say the hieroglyphics in this tomb represent a sort of posthumous shopping list, it's all the things that the priest who's buried here wants his 18 children to buy him once he's dead. But others want to know not only what was said, but how it was said. One researcher believes music is the key. Classical violinist Mohammed Musiret says that by comparing written Egyptian lyrics with Coptic songs of today, he has been able to approximate the music of the pharaohs.

Man 3: Something like that.

Man 2: We don't really know the sounds of all the words and we'll never know.

Reporter: So the language may be lost forever, but not the meaning. An example, this newly discovered text says, "If you break into my tomb, you'll be eaten by a crocodile, a lion, and a hippopotamus." We get the message.

Chapter 3   Pedal Power

Useful Vocabulary

Gilligan's Island: an American television comedy drama in which a group of people on a desert island have to improvise in order to survive

pedal-powered: powered by the motion of pedaling, like a bicycle

a prototype: a model of an object, used for testing before the final product is made

a device: a tool, machine, or invention

bush: wild forest, grassland, or desert, without any settlements

portable: able to be carried

durable: strong, long-lasting

to refine: to improve; to make perfect

to take for a spin: to take for a short drive; (here) to give something a try

Reporter: It's an invention straight out of a *Gilligan's Island* episode—a pedal-powered washing machine. This prototype device was developed as a final-year project by two mechanical engineering students from the Royal Melbourne Institute of Technology in Australia. The washer is a labor-saving device for people in developing countries who wash their clothes by hand. Institute administrators say it could even be used closer to home by people in the Australian bush.

Student: Our machine uses the pedaling motion, because the major part of the power comes from the muscles of the legs. This can also be a form of exercise for the people there.

Reporter: Besides not requiring electricity, the washer also doesn't need to be connected to a water supply. The students say the washer is environmentally friendly, portable, and its simple design makes it easy to repair. It's made from cheap but durable materials, and the Institute believes the washers could be manufactured for about thirty dollars.

Institute Administrator: We need to get someone who will look at it, who will refine it, talk to some of the communities about their needs to make sure it's appropriate, and then, of course, manufacture it.

Reporter: Administrators say the next step is to find a community to test the washer under real-world conditions. But they think they'll have no problem finding someone willing to take this pedal-powered washer for a spin.

Chapter 4	CITES Conference on Endangered Species

Useful Vocabulary
seahorse: a small bony fish that looks like a horse
haggling: arguing
flora and fauna: all the plants and animals in a specific area or time period
ivory: the hard, white substance of an elephant's tusks
poachers: people who hunt animals illegally
logging: the industry of cutting down trees for wood products

Reporter: The world is now a safer place for some creatures of the sea—the two largest species of fish and seahorses—but there may be a new threat facing elephants in Africa and Asia. It's the outcome of two weeks of intense haggling and final voting by some 160 member nations at the CITES conference in Santiago, Chile. CITES is the Convention on International Trade in Endangered Species of wild flora and fauna, the main international body that regulates trade in endangered wildlife.

The meeting adopted several hotly debated measures affecting commercial fishing interests, and for the first time it has given protection to sharks. Whale sharks and basking sharks are declining worldwide, hunted for their meat and fins. International commercial trade in these fish will now be allowed only with strictly controlled permits. The same protection was given to all species of seahorses, many of them overexploited for use in traditional medicines and the aquarium trade.

Among the wildlife also given new protection, twenty-six species of Asian turtles and the Black Sea's population of bottle-nosed dolphins, decisions welcomed by wildlife conservationists. But some say the meeting made a risky decision by giving conditional approval to three southern African nations to sell their large stockpiles of elephant ivory. Opponents of the sales argue only a total ban on the ivory trade, enforced since 1989, will discourage poachers from killing elephants.

Another major decision—after many years of debate, new trade controls on South American mahogany, a valuable hardwood rapidly disappearing due to widespread illegal logging. The measure was opposed by furniture manufacturers in the United States, the biggest importer of South American mahogany. The next CITES conference will be held in two years in Thailand.

Chapter 5	Psychology Exhibit

Useful Vocabulary

Smithsonian: a national museum and research center of art, history, culture, science and technology, located in Washington, D.C.
an illusion: something that misleads or deceives
diversity: variety
breadth: wide range
light-hearted: not serious
voyeurism: the act of getting pleasure from secretly watching others

Reporter: A rotating tent fools this man into thinking he's moving. An ancient Chinese civil service exam requires drawing a square with the left hand while drawing a circle with the right. A modern challenge asks this woman to concentrate on the colors and ignore the words. It's all part of the Smithsonian's look at the mind-boggling world of psychology—a dizzying array of illuminating illusions that can make a visitor's head spin. And that's just what the American Psychological Association had in mind when it developed the exhibit.

APA Spokesperson: Science museums by and large have neglected psychology. There have been a few scattered things, but nothing that attempts to portray the breadth and diversity of psychology.

Reporter: Couples can discover if they are more cooperative or combative in a psychological tug of war. Children are invited to look inward by drawing self-portraits in chalk. In this simple experiment, visitors are told to walk only on the black squares. Most do, demonstrating how the psychological principles of authority and the power of the situation can result in blind obedience. At the end of the checkerboard walkway, a display attempts to explain why good people are capable of evil acts. A video display shows controversial experiments from the 1960s in which researchers found that two thirds of volunteers would give what they thought were severe electric shocks to others, simply because they were told to. But mostly the exhibits are light-hearted mind games, such as a test of eye-hand response time.

Adult Visitor: Museums are wonderful, but in this kind of museum you can do things, like even my parents are acting like little kids.

Child Visitor: It's very interesting and you can learn a lot, but have fun at the same time.

Reporter: In fact, the visitors are part of the exhibit.

Curator: The exhibition in some way encourages an interesting kind of voyeurism, because as people are exploring their own responses to the exhibition components, other people are watching them and analyzing those kinds of responses and interactions that they're having.

Reporter: Organizers hope as the exhibition travels around the U.S. it will bring with it a greater insight into the many facets of human psychology.

Useful Vocabulary
catchword: slogan
a bridle: (here) a leather strap on a shoe
precarious: unstable; not safe
to rip off: to take advantage of by charging too much money; (here) to steal
know-how: practical knowledge
exotic: unusual

Reporter: Beauty, of course, is in the eye of the beholder, but when it comes to footwear, everyone agrees it can either make or break one's entire image. "Choose your shoes" was the catchword of this young designer's stand—interchangeable straps, or bridles, as they're known in the business. Getting a reputation, for some, is the point of the exercise. "It's my first collection; I have to get a name," says Vietnamese-born Vu Yuen Kee. His shoes feature heels precariously situated, bordering, he admitted, on the impractical.

Designer 1: This is one of my particular favorites. The shapes and colors were inspired by the night sky.

Reporter: Young Clare Singleton, from Britain and barely out of fashion school, hopes to get noticed, but knows there are risks.

Designer 1: People at a show, especially like this, can come around and, well, rip you off, really. But it's a chance you have to take.

Reporter: Well-established companies, like Charles Jourdan, hire about twenty promising designers every year, guiding them towards producing footwear that sells.

Company Spokesperson: Obviously, here there are products you can't sell. It's a good idea, but you can't sell it. So, people have to come, they have the technical know-how, and those people will make, from an idea, they will make something wearable.

Reporter: Twenty-three-year-old Isabel Borgie is French, Algerian, and Indonesian. She uses products as exotic as her background: stingray fish skin, cocoon silks, and semi-precious stones. These, made with amethysts, sell for about $200 a pair.

Designer 2: I already have something like fifteen orders from around the world, in French, Italy, German, Japan, and all Europe, not yet in America.

| Chapter 7 | Organic Food Labels |

Useful Vocabulary
a booming market: a successful market that is growing
organics: foods that are grown naturally
to compare apples and oranges: to try to compare things that cannot be compared because they are so different
USDA: United States Department of Agriculture
to ban: to prohibit or forbid
irradiated: treated with radiation to kill germs or substances that cause diseases
conventional: traditional; (here) chemical
synthetic: artificial; biochemically produced; not organic

Reporter: It's a booming market, but consumers often admit, shopping for organics is like comparing apples and oranges. For years, states set their own criteria.

Shopper 1: What I want is organic food, and I think many people don't have time to read labels or make assumptions that may not be true.

Reporter: Under the new USDA guidelines, organic food cannot be irradiated or genetically altered. Most conventional pesticides and synthetic fertilizers are also banned, and products like meat cannot contain any hormones or antibiotics. New USDA seals will assure shoppers that a product is at least 95% organic. Anything less will either say "Made with organic ingredients" on the front panel or have those organic items listed on the back.

Store Manager: The certification process does not make any claims that organic food is better for you; what certification does is it verifies that those products have been grown in accordance with the organic standards.

Reporter: Many say a national standard is long overdue. Consumers, who pay on average 10 to 50 percent more for organic goods, say they will now have more confidence in the products they buy.

Shopper 2: You don't have to think of it quite as much. You kind of know what you're getting, and you trust what you're getting.

Reporter: Making shopping for organics a whole lot easier.

Chapter 8	Better Lives for Chickens

Useful Vocabulary
a perch: a place where a bird sits or rests
rafters: beams, usually made of wood, that support a roof
to roost: to rest or sleep (generally used when referring to birds)
a henhouse: shelter where hens roost and lay eggs
to boost: to increase
hare-brained: silly; foolish
off-the-wall: uncommon; crazy
a trend: a reoccurring pattern

Chicken Farmer: They have perches, they can get up, they can get up and roost in the rafters, they can get up in the nests. And it's really important to a chicken, so I've been told by researchers, to have a nest to lay her eggs in.

Reporter: The most important difference between the chickens here at this farm near Hudson and most major egg producers is what you don't see. There are no cages for the birds. They're free to wander around the henhouse here, stretch their wings, and socialize. Cyd says she's not here to put the big egg producers out of business. To give you an idea of the difference in size, if these birds were all caged, 75,000 would fit inside this henhouse. As it is, there are only 5,500 in here. There are other differences here too. Cyd Styron doesn't use any pesticides or antibiotics to boost egg production. She says the idea of humane egg production isn't so far out anymore, even though her family thought she was crazy to try it here in Colorado.

Chicken Farmer: So this isn't some hare-brained, off-the-wall, blond scheme that, you know, we came up with, but it's actually a trend that's happening in other countries.

Reporter: Styron says some European countries already ban cages. Even with antiquated equipment and only nine employees, the business of Colorado Natural Eggs has grown 300 percent in the last year, but that's not to say a carton of eggs is cheap. Because the small operation is labor-intensive, and the chickens actually produce fewer eggs, these cost about a dollar more than other store-bought eggs.

Chicken Farmer: People who have a commitment to their own health and to the welfare of animals—they probably mind paying more, but they're willing to make the sacrifice because they have a commitment.

Reporter: Styron says as more people become aware of the way most farm animals are typically treated, she expects more competition in the humane-farming community. It'll be better for the chickens, she says, and better for the humans who eat their eggs.

Chapter 9	The New Globe Theatre

Useful Vocabulary

a rubbish dump: a place where trash or garbage or disposed of
to pay tribute: to honor
glittering: shiny and bright
reign: the time a king or queen rules
the McCarthy era: a period of extreme anti-Communist politics in the United States
replica: something made to look exactly like the original
rowdy and rambunctious: unruly and difficult to control
Puritans: members of a Protestant religious group of the 16th and 17th centuries who believed strictly in doctrine and disapproved of public entertainments

Reporter: In 1985, the local government bought a rubbish dump, which seems more appropriate and more useful on this site than an authentic Shakespearean theater. Hence, Sam Wanamaker saw his dream, already reeling from fifteen years of setbacks, again slipping away.

Wanamaker: It is a horrible omission on the part of a culture-conscious nation that represents the highest cultural ideas of Western civilization not to pay tribute in some memorial, monumental sense to the greatest playwright Western civilization has ever known.

Reporter: On Thursday, Sam's dream finally came to glittering life. Queen Elizabeth II arrived in style to honor the artist who graced the reign of Queen Elizabeth I four centuries ago. Wanamaker, a Hollywood filmmaker who moved to England during the McCarthy era, did not live to see this moment. His actress daughter Zoe recalls what he had to overcome.

Zoe: People felt that we didn't need another theater, but I think we always need theaters.

Reporter: The original Globe, where Shakespeare and his company put on *King Lear, Romeo and Juliet,* and *Othello,* burned down in 1613 and was immediately rebuilt. The site was discovered just around the corner from the replica in 1989, confirmed by the layer of burned wood and the litter from nut-crunching playgoers. The new Globe is founded on modern concrete and steel, but finished with methods and materials of the first Elizabethan age, adapted to modern safety laws. It took around six years in all. Sam Wanamaker lived to see construction well under way. In 1993, not long before his death, an improvised performance by the first professional group to trod a Globe stage in more than three hundred and fifty years. The theater was rowdy and rambunctious in Elizabethan times— the audience wandered out to get a beer, crunched their snacks, offered their comments, and threw things at players they didn't like.

Wanamaker: Everyone had a jolly good time, as they say. And that's what we want to revive.

Reporter: The Puritans shut down the Globe in 1642, but they couldn't keep it closed.